THE TRUTH
BEYOND
WHAT
IS

THE TRUTH BEYOND WHAT IS

Marie Poirier

BALBOA
PRESS

A DIVISION OF HAY HOUSE

Balboa Press books may be ordered through booksellers or by contacting:

Balboa Press
A Division of Hay House
1663 Liberty Drive
Bloomington, IN 47403
www.balboapress.com
1 (877) 407-4847

Because of the dynamic nature of the Internet, any web addresses or links contained in this book may have changed since publication and may no longer be valid. The views expressed in this work are solely those of the author and do not necessarily reflect the views of the publisher, and the publisher hereby disclaims any responsibility for them.

The author of this book does not dispense medical advice or prescribe the use of any technique as a form of treatment for physical, emotional, or medical problems without the advice of a physician, either directly or indirectly. The intent of the author is only to offer information of a general nature to help you in your quest for emotional and spiritual well-being. In the event you use any of the information in this book for yourself, which is your constitutional right, the author and the publisher assume no responsibility for your actions.

Any people depicted in stock imagery provided by Thinkstock are models, and such images are being used for illustrative purposes only.
Certain stock imagery © Thinkstock.

Print information available on the last page.

ISBN: 978-1-5043-3890-5 (sc)
ISBN: 978-1-5043-3891-2 (e)

Balboa Press rev. date: 10/1/2015

Dedicated to my Daughter
Eve-Alexandra
2000-2013
The Power of Her Beauty, Her Purity,
and Her Wisdom, flows within me for Eternity.

Acknowledgments

My Highest Gratitude

For the gratitude that I feel toward the great teachers that led me to the beginning of my powerful journey, and for the knowledge which I hold, I thank you from the core of my being. To Jerry and Esther Hicks and their teachings, whom I feel to be the greatest and most powerful teachers of mankind; Rhonda Byrne for her fascinating writings; the creator of Igetrealtv, Scott Ercoliani for his powerful teachings through his videos; Jon Mercer for his uplifting work; Bob Proctor for his powerful messages; Mark Hamilton for his movement to create positive change; and visionary Michael Beck for the powerful passion that he holds. Never has there been a human upon this planet who held so much passion and helped so many children as for Michael Jackson, through his power of love that he held no matter how many lies were created toward him, from societies tabloids for the purpose of their own agenda, as many overlooked the positive impact he had on so many children upon this planet. His power inspired me a great deal. These are but a few of the powerful creators who have touched the lives of so many.

Much love to my angelic daughter Eve-Alexandra, whose wisdom and purity is always a part of me; my friend Colette Gibbins for being a great example of keeping a positive outlook in life no matter what obstacles we encountered; Shanna O'Brien for her support and understanding; my beautiful and wise cat Amigo who is a great energy balancer and how grateful I am for Balboa Press who are sharing their kindness, magnificent support, time and positive energy towards helping me publish my writing.

No words can explain my gratitude toward the teachings I've received from all those magnificent creators and all the people that I've met throughout my life's journey and most of all, my gratitude toward the purest Source of positive energy that flows through me for the messages that I write.

I thank you all for being part of my experience.

Contents

Introduction: Entering The Journey

From the powers of the Universe itself, welcome to the truth and nothing but the truth which is revealed within _The Truth Beyond What Is_. You shall experience and know the truth, for it shall resonate within you in a powerful way as the powers of the Universe rush through your every cell. You will feel as though you are beginning a journey toward a new world. Your wanting has begun this journey, for to evolve and to keep evolving is the natural state of being for humans. If not, you wouldn't be part of this physical existence.

It is no accident that this book has made its way into the hands of those who are asking for change.

There are no words strong enough to emphasize the extreme importance for you to understand the following. Once you begin this powerful journey within _The Truth Beyond What Is_, you can never go back, because you will never want to go back. One can describe this journey as the opening of the doorway through the rabbit hole, leading toward the passage to the world of the unknown. I am not writing to convince you of its truth, I am only writing the truth as it is.

Some may condemn these words. Some will ponder these words. Some may find their awareness and clarity of its knowledge and there will be those who shall find and hold the key to master their powers.

It is my powerful knowing that if this knowledge was ever to be taught in schools, other than basic writing, reading and calculating, it would be the only knowledge of truth that the children would ever need to know to become the powerful geniuses that they are for, they came forth to create a life of growth, freedom and joy. It must be. It is law so it shall be.

It is my intent to write the words that flow through me for those who are asking for change.

Part One

The Truth Beyond The Great Awakening

What is the Great Awakening? It is a time where you regain your powers. A time you feel enlightened, feel unlimited abundance, pure joy, and freedom. It is a time you awaken to the remembering of *who you really are* and with the powers you really hold. It is a powerful shift, not only a planetary shift but a consciousness shift that will touch and have an impact on every single human upon this planet. Those who will align with this shift shall thrive. There may be those who will fight against its harmony whom in return shall be guided with great emotional messages, which they shall feel a discord within the core of their being, who may be led to confusion experiencing powerful disparity, leading them to reemerge to *who they really are.*

The Nine Stages Of The Great Awakening

The mastery of the Great Awakening consists of nine powerful stages.

Every stage will find its way closer to your powerful remembering of *who you really are* and of the powers that you hold. These stages will evolve naturally, for these processes are guided by a force that is bigger than the world itself. The only differences that will occur, there will be those who shall allow it to happen and those who shall fight against its nature. Either way, all humans upon the planet shall be touched within this time of the great awakening.

In the pages that follow, I shall explain the different stages. My written thoughts on these stages shall be short and to the core of its truth.

First Stage: The Desire For Freedom

In this stage more than ever, you shall hold a powerful desire for freedom, which is the normal process of the first stage.

The institutions of schools, the churches, the rules of medicine for physical and mental health, and the obedience of thy parents, in other words, the rules and laws of man which are programmed into the human race as the beliefs of the realities that they shall face. It is those who lived by these rules who shall feel the greatest desire for freedom due to the discord they feel within themselves for obeying the false beliefs created by man.

Second Stage: The Questioning

As you have lived your life by the rules of man, you may strongly feel a sense that life just isn't working out for you. You may begin to question life itself. Your unknowing to life's purpose shall want answers.

What is my purpose and why am I here? Why the suffering? Why do I feel trapped when I should be happy? What is life about? Why is life such a struggle? Why is life so hard? What am I doing wrong? Why are the dollars so hard to come by? Why do I feel so tired? Why? Why? Why?

Third Stage: The Quest For Answers

You may begin to feel that something about life just isn't right, and as you do, you'll begin searching the world to find the answers. Most will commonly turn to numerous religions which are created and written by man, preaching rules that you must sacrifice, suffer, give up your desires for money and material possessions, and go without to find peace. Some may preach their beliefs that you have a price to pay for happiness and you must prove yourself worthy to make it to heaven's gate.

But then again, after feeling great discord within oneself and still looking for answers, some may turn to more education, again having to prove themselves worthy by being graded for their knowledge of what was taught, and led to believe that the only way to bring in the dollars from their taught knowledge is to struggle and become competitive. You must compete to get ahead. You must compete for the position. You must compete for the dollars. In other words, again you must compete to prove yourself worthy because it is a competitive world and it is the only way to bring in the dollars. You must work hard even drive yourself to the ground at times, with work that you are not happy with, believing it is the only way for survival and comfort. Because of your competitive world, you are convinced of the importance to be kept informed of the world around you through addiction to the media, which will make you believe that there is a shortage of food or a shortage of water, keeping you aware of how bad things are in the world and of the upcoming depression of the economy and so on.

Now you are faced with the horrors of life, your survival, the constant struggle, and the bills that are piling up that need to be paid. Due to a continued discord you feel within yourself, again your search for answers returns. By this time, you are led to believe that financial freedom is the answer, and you are determined to experience freedom through self-employment. You now believe that being your own boss is the only answer to a happy life. So you now have your own business, working a hundred times harder and becoming even more competitive. Exhausted by your determination to succeed, you have now reached the success of the dollars. You keep looking over your shoulder due to your competitive mind, constantly working harder as you are worried for your company's continuance and about losing everything that you worked for. You now find yourself in a state of exhaustion.

If you believe that a life of struggle and hardship is what life on earth is all about, perhaps preparing your grave now would be a good idea. One must wonder as to why the life-insurance industry is making a killing. This industry must know exactly who to target.

As you are led further into discouragement, you conclude that you have tried everything to make your life work in your favor. This is the time you will want to begin blaming others for your world as it is.

Fourth Stage: The Shocking Truth

Determination leads you to find the truth as to what or who is to blame for all your world's obstacles. Though, you do not have the means to travel the world, your next logical step to continue your search will most likely be the world's library, the internet. You then search the internet for similarities from those who have traveled the same path of the journey, those who are also in despair.

Like most have found, to your surprise, you shall discover that it all began at birth. You discover the facts that the mass population is under a system of control by a small few who believe they own the planet. As you dig further into your search, you will develop a strong belief that you are now powerless as this control over you has begun from your birth, at the institution you call a hospital, where the registration of a birth certificate introduced you into this system of control. Then you may come to realize that you like most, have been lied to all your life, through the controlled systems of schools, religions, doctors, neighbors, friends, thy mighty parents and by all of life's societies in general.

The blame for all your despair shall reveal itself at its deepest level possible at this stage of The Shocking Truth. But later, you will not condemn those beings, as you will become aware that they too are blinded by the system of control, since they believe they are doing the right thing according to their programmed beliefs.

Fifth Stage: The Threshold Before The Light: The Need To Fix The World

As your truth has finally revealed itself as to what or who is to blame, you may now come to the conclusion that you are powerless and that the world is broken. Through this stage, from the emotions of despair, fear, anger and revenge, you shall crave the need to fix the broken world in order to gain the powers of your greatest desires which are to finally feel worthy, deserving, happy and most of all, to have your freedom. You may then feel a strong belief that coming forth to this planet was your calling, which your purpose or your mission is to fix the broken world and to save its people.

With your rebellious determination to make the world a better place, it shall then get you further into your struggle to fight for the world, fight for the planet, fight for its people, and fight for the animals or whichever other cause you may need to fight for, unaware that you will feel angrier and even more vengeful. Then one shall find themselves further within powerlessness through emotional exhaustion, yet stronger than ever before.

Sixth Stage: The Letting Go

There is something of great importance you will experience in this stage. You will begin to feel that *fear is not real*, that fear is only an illusion. You shall realize that fear is the trigger for anger, despair, revenge, sadness, disappointment, the feeling of lack and any feeling of discord you may feel within yourself. You will start to realize that fear is but a cleverly designed system fabricated and created by man, for the purpose of control over the consciousness of the mass population.

It shall resonate with you that fear *is not real*, that it is only an illusion. You will ask yourself, what is an emotion? And you shall realize that it is not visible, that you can't see it, smell it, hear it, taste it or touch it. Then you will ask yourself; what is fear? And you shall realize that fear is an emotion, an illusion and therefore, *not real*.

You will begin to realize, fear is only a state of emotion brought on by your very own thoughts you chose to think. Your thoughts are always in harmony with the emotions that you feel. If you were told that fear is all in the mind, you will know that fear is all in the way you feel, a feeling brought on and started by a thought.

You shall realize that as you think, you feel an emotion. Thoughts and emotions can never be separated. One cannot exist without the other. It's the same for every physical human upon this planet. There are no exceptions.

This stage will be the time that you want to let go, the time to free yourself; to let go all fear and all doubt; to make room for the truth of the powers that you really hold; to let go and let the powers of the Universe help remind you what was rightfully yours; to free your mind to align with the powers of the Universe which are the same powers you were born with.

As this resonates with you, you will want to believe that you came forth to this physical planet as powerful and not just to fend for yourself. You didn't come here powerless. If that were the case, you would never have been able to figure out why you are here and why you chose to come here, as you will come to know. You shall know that you had these powers before you came to this physical world, as you used your powers to get here. If not, you would not be here. You will know, you did not come forth to suffer and struggle. You will know, you eagerly and joyfully chose to come forth into this magnificent physical world with the powers that you hold, to create with your thoughts and powers which are guided by your system of emotions, which are guiding you on your path toward a life of growth, freedom and joy for becoming, for doing and for having anything you desire, *effortlessly*.

Seventh Stage: The Awareness And Clarity

After wanting to let go and release all fears, in this stage, you shall be led into a journey to find great awareness and clarity. It will be no accident that you shall be led to the knowledge that shall inspire you with the eye-opening journey of *The Truth Beyond What Is.*

You shall hold the awareness that fighting for the world and for the people was only contributing towards the growth of the problems you were facing. You shall hold the awareness that as you were fighting against the bad, you were actually feeding the bad. In this stage, you shall gain the knowledge that everything is energy and your fighting was feeding energy to the wrong. You will become aware that feeding bad energy will only feed those within that same energy. You shall gain the awareness and clarity of how similar frequencies of energy are attracted to each other, which perpetuates the energy in a powerful way.

You shall hold the awareness and clarity that releasing all fear, anger, revenge and fighting is the key to make yourself invisible and non-existent to those negative illusions that you were feeding, contributing to their stronger growth and *you shall become more powerful than they will ever be.*

Eighth Stage: The Knowledge Of Who You Really Are

In this magnificent stage you shall know, you did not come forth on a mission to fix a world that is broken. You shall know the world is in perfect harmony. You shall know the illusion of time is for the purpose of your own creation. You shall know the disparity you've experienced was to your benefit but could have been prevented. You shall laugh at the fact you chose to trap yourself within that disparity, now that you are aware it was but an illusion, an illusion for the purpose of your creations and growth. You shall know you alone and no one else were to blame for all the obstacles that you've experienced.

You shall hold the awareness that environmental issues are overrated and exaggerated, due to planet Earth's own power of consciousness and it is prepared with anything it needs within its own natural force. Your knowing that you can be, do and have absolutely anything you desire, shall be clear to you.

You shall know how powerful you really are. You shall know who you really are, where you came from, why you chose to come forth, your purpose for being here and where you go after leaving this physical world, as you shall be aware that there is no such thing as death.

You shall know the powers of your own thoughts and the importance of your emotions, as they are guiding you. You shall be aware that you are the creator of your own world and you have the power to live in a most beautiful and magnificent reality with the freedom to choose whatever you want to create.

Ninth Stage: The Remembering Of Who You Really Are

In this stage, you shall travel beyond the unknown in a powerful journey to the remembering of *who you really are*. Your life as it is, and your future as you will create it to be, shall be known by you in the now. Life shall no longer be a mystery to you.

You shall hold unconditional love for yourself. You shall remember that there is nothing more important in the entire Universe than to feel good. You shall feel that you have finally awakened from a coma. You shall feel like you've been struck by lightning with powerful energy. You shall thrive. You shall finally be living the life of growth, freedom and joy for which you are so worthy and so deserving of.

You shall hold the key to be, to do and to have anything that you desire, effortlessly. And with this key that you hold, you shall master its powers. You are the powerful-pure-intentional genius creator that you chose to come forth into this magnificent realm to be. Not only shall you *know thyself,* but you shall *remember who you really are.*

A Note In Closing

The awareness of the illusion that the world is in a dysfunctional state, is not in itself, the great awakening, though many believe it to be. This knowledge is only an early stage, and it is of great importance that one must not trap themselves within such knowledge.

The truth *beyond* that threshold is the awakening to *who you really are,* which in truth; is the powerful nature of the great awakening.

Part Two

Knowing The Energy That You Are

A very small portion of what you are within this physical realm, is a magnificent physical machine, an apparatus, with physical senses that are interpreters of vibrating energy for the purpose of feeling the tangibility of form within the physical realm. It is a highly sophisticated piece of machinery and cleverly designed with perfection.

This machine that you have has the ability to interpret language for the purpose of communicating with other bodily machines. When this machine stops operating, which most call the death experience; it is no different than burying a dead leaf as it is only another physical material that is used to be part of this physical realm. You do not die. The machine you were using to operate through just stopped functioning, but *you* did not.

This magnificent machine is not who you really are. It is only a material thing that you have as part of this material world, so when someone tells you how wrong it is to be materialistic, they cannot possibly be happy within their own skin due to the fact, that they are themselves materialistic in form. In other words, every material thing on this planet is in physical form. We are all materialistic by definition due to our physical form or body.

There is no difference in what we call the material world or physical world. Again, this machine or body that you carry with you every day is only something, a thing that you are temporarily using and operating within, because operating through a material form was the only way to enter into this physical world.

So you see, your body is not who you really are. It is only a machine you are temporarily using to be inside of for this physical experience. You must place yourself inside a physical machine to enter this physical realm. It is only something you are inside of, for your joyful experience within this material or physical realm.

The truth of who you really are is *within* your physical body, but you cannot be described as physical form yourself, because who you really are is invisible to the seeing eye, nor can you be seen through an x-ray. You are not something physical that you can see, because who you are is non-physical and who you are is something you can only *feel*. When you feel, it is not just a feeling, it is you. You are energy and consciousness.

The energy that you are, is 100% positive and at its purest level. You are energy that is so powerful that no words are able to describe the equivalency of its strength.

Most people's logic will use the word energy to describe a performance or a movement. The faster a physical object moves, the more energy it has and the slower the object moves, the less energy it has. The energy that you are is also movement in a performance of vibration. The frequency of your vibration is so fast and so powerful that if one could see this energy, he would see its stream penetrate right through the Universe. One cannot see this stream, but if one was to go within, they shall feel its power; which is *who they really are.*

To further explain who you are, is to explain that you are not only vibrating energy, but conscious energy, *energy which is thought or thinking energy.* The thinking part of energy is what creates the level of frequency; frequency defined as the speed of its vibration.

Thought and energy are not separate. It cannot be one or the other because it is part of the same design, it is *one.* Thought is energy and energy is thought and the frequency determines the level or the power and speed of its movement. Therefore, you are *thought energy.* The *thought energy* that you are is so powerful, if you go within and feel it, you shall hold an awareness of the powerful being that you really are.

It is important for you to know and I cannot emphasize enough, that manmade IQ testing cannot determine ones' genius abilities. IQ testing is for the purpose of analyzing humans to see whether or not they have been properly programmed within the rules of society. Your natural genius abilities are so advanced that no man on earth can possibly analyze its true nature with a manmade written IQ test.

Knowing The Energy That You Came From

An understanding of the energy that you really are, which is focused within the physical realm, shall give you a better understanding of where you came from.

Before your arrival on earth, you were no different than you are now, in the exception that you were not in physical form inside a physical body. You were in a non-physical state, the same as you are now, but invisible to the eyes of humans on earth.

So let's say that here on earth you were to come out of the body that you are inside of, you would still be who you are, but you would be invisible to other humans. You came forth from another realm which is an invisible realm. It is where you created yourself within the image in your thought, creating the physical body you came forth into.

The non-physical world, from which you came, is not really a place that you can point your finger at, because it is not in visible form. It's like an awareness or an existence. It cannot be seen. It can only be felt. In the non-physical world, you cannot be created or destroyed because you have no beginning or ending. You always were, you always are and you always will be, but you are a creator and you have the ability and the power to transform or change any or all of your creations.

The non-physical world is where you are established now and it will always be your real home and your only purpose for existence is for the purpose of creating. It is also the head office where all of your creations from thought energy start taking place.

You are energy. You are consciousness. You are creator. You are worthy. You are loved. You are naturally powerful and you are governed by Universal laws and agreements for the purpose of maintaining your existence and your thought creations in perfect balance and harmony. There are absolutely no words that I can use to describe the magnificence of that which you are.

Below are just a few examples of the differences between the non-physical world that you came from and the physical world that you are now experiencing.

- The physical world has a law of gravity. Its purpose is to keep physical objects grounded. Without gravity everything would be floating. Your Energy also harmonizes within this law, as your energy which is you, reacts to the magnetic field. Therefore, the Energy that you are is magnetized.

  The non-physical world has no need for gravity because there are no physical objects to hold in place. Everything exists in conscious non-physical state.

- The physical world has the law of time for the purpose of creation. Many humans are confused about its real purpose. The true purpose for time shall be described in greater detail in Part Five.

  The non-physical world has no measurement of time. It cannot be measured, calculated or physically traveled because it has no beginning and no ending. It has no past or future. It always exists in the now.

The saying "life is short" is correct. A fifty year life experience in the physical world is equivalent to maybe a few minutes or even seconds in the non-physical world. That's why you've been coming back thousands of times. So if you think you are old, think again. Your life here on earth is much shorter than you think.

You are programmed to believe the illusions of a reality in which you are getting older and weaker. As one knows his true powers of *who they really are*, one can look and feel twenty as they think they are approaching seventy, eighty or ninety.

Time is irrelevant. Time is something of an illusion once you understand its true nature. It is commonly being utilized contrary to its own purpose. By the time you finish reading this book, your understanding of the true purpose of time will be of greater clarity to you.

- In the physical world, you require sleep for the purpose of releasing all resistance and the emotions of disparity from your conscious thinking, as you reconnect back home to your non-physical world. The only purpose for sleep is to place your illusions of the physical reality on pause, releasing all resistance and disparity.

In the non-physical world, you do not sleep because you have no resistance or disparity to release. It is only pure positive energy which you are.

- In your physical world, you have emotions which are a guiding system designed for your existence in the physical realm, monitoring the frequency level of the energy that you are operating on. When you are feeling good, you are vibrating at a high frequency level which is an indicator that you are in your natural state. When you are feeling bad, your guidance kicks in to indicate that your frequency level is too low which is unnatural to your existence, that's why you feel that discord within the being that you are.

The emotional guiding system is for the purpose of guiding you here in the physical realm, giving you indication to whether your frequency is at its natural level or if you are trapping yourself within the illusions of the physical world, known to you as feeling bad. Before you came into the physical realm, you made sure that you were prepared to be guided here so you can function in your natural state, which is pure powerful energy. In Part Three, you shall read more of this powerful system or your invisible GPS (Global Positioning System) as I call it, which is connected within you and started operating the day you entered the physical world.

Your non-physical world has no need for an emotional guiding system because it consists only of pure positive energy. In your non-physical world, you are always in your natural state which is well-being, joy, love, and all-powerful. There is no need to be guided in the right track because resistance or disparity is not recognized in the non-physical world. It does not exist there.

- In your physical world, you are flowing in separate physical bodies which hold different perspectives to create in fast motion forward.

  In the non-physical world, you are all *one* energy and consciousness.

- In the physical world, you have no recollection of your past lives, for good reason.

  In the non-physical world, you have recollection of all your past lives.

- In the physical world, you have your senses which are hearing, seeing, smelling, tasting and touching.

  In the non-physical world, you have no physical senses because you are not in physical form, but you do communicate perfectly and more powerfully through the vibrations of your energy.

Here are three important things that are similar:

- The non-physical world operates from *thinking energy*.

  The physical world also operates from the exact same *thinking energy*.

- The non-physical world is governed by Universal Laws.

  The physical world is also governed by the exact same Universal Laws, but most humans don't align with them.

- In the non-physical world, you are *powerful genius creators* with your natural energy of love and appreciations, meaning you are in a natural state of thriving.

In the physical world, you are also *powerful genius creators* with your natural energy of love, appreciation, thriving and well-being, only most humans don't remember who they really are. That's why you feel the discord within your physical body as feeling bad when you are not in your natural state.

Knowing Your Purpose And Mission

Your birth was no accident. It was your own joyful choice to come forth. You have a purpose and a mission for being here and once you reach the clarity of why you came forth into this physical world, it is my absolute promise to you that you shall feel the worthiness of your being here.

You existed long before you came here to this physical world, and you've been here thousands of times by your own choice. It is for good reason that you do not remember your past lives, because motion forward is the order of the Universe and you must trust that life is designed in perfect balance and harmony with the Laws of the Universe. If you were to focus back, you could never move forward. It would be like getting into your vehicle and driving backwards; you would never get to your destination. So be grateful that you do not remember your past lives and you do not want to waste your time trying to remember them, because it is of no benefit to your future. If it was of any importance for you to remember, you would have come forth remembering.

Some may believe that there is a karma that they did something wrong in their past life and that's the reason they are suffering now. That cliché belief has caused humans to believe that they are here to fix themselves. That belief only leads to confusion. You must release that belief. You did not come forth to fix yourself or to fix the world and what you are living now has nothing to do with your past lives.

Before you came forth, you knew that the physical world was a world that contained disparity, that's why you were prepared before you came. Some may question as to why they would choose to come into a world of disparity or contrast. You knew then, the disparity was for the purpose of your joyous motion forward to perfect your creations.

You knew then, you were not coming into a world of disparity to experience disparity and you knew that if you were to disconnect and lose yourself within its illusions, that the disparity would be a fast motion forward to get yourself back on track, knowing that it cannot harm you because it is an illusion. You knew then, the emotional system you were coming forth with was to prevent you from trapping yourself within the illusions of disparity. You knew of your powerful genius abilities to create and that the physical world is a place to create anything you desired in its physical form. You knew you could be, do and have anything you choose. You knew this was a world of freedom and you can never go wrong.

Close your eyes and visualize a beautiful tree. As you can see it in your visual thought, it actually exists, but the difference is that it is not in physical form. It only exists in the non-physical realm. But it still exists. So, you can imagine the excitement you felt coming forth into this physical world; by using your physical senses, you can actually see and touch the tree, smell the aroma and taste its delicious fruit, as it is in its physical form.

Do you see how fortunate you are to be here? Many are not aware of their powerful experience. How grateful I am to be here in this magnificent physical world.

How eager you were to come forth, but in order to come forth one had to be a powerful creative genius. It is the only way you can come forth into this physical realm.

So, do you realize how powerful you are? Do you realize how worthy you are? You do not have to prove yourself worthy to anyone. You are here because you are powerful. You are here because of the worthiness that you are. Do not think for one minute that you are powerless or unworthy due to others' opinion, for themselves, they do not hold an awareness of *who they really are*. You are worthy and powerful just because you exist here. If you weren't worthy and powerful, you would not have been able to get yourself here. You are worthy and powerful just for existing in the physical world.

What is your purpose for being here? You are thought energy and the function of thought is to create, which is the reason that you are a natural built-in creator, sort of like a natural built-in creating machine. That is what thought energy is, but it can only operate and function properly in its natural state of purity, which is the energy that you are. The only purpose that you chose to come forth into this physical world is to create and the only mission you intended to be on, is a mission of joy. Whether you believe this or not, it is the absolute truth.

Do you actually believe that one would willingly and joyfully choose to come forth in the physical world to suffer and struggle? It is very important that you question that at your deepest level. Why would you ever think for a moment, that you would choose to come forth into a world to suffer and struggle? Do you actually believe you would come here powerless, in this magnificent world of diversity?

Another reason you chose to come forth, is because you had the power and the freedom to choose to create anything you desire and there wouldn't be any right or wrong choices. You did not choose to come to this physical world to suffer or struggle. You alone by your choice, chose to suffer and struggle and if you are, it is because you lost yourself somewhere within your physical journey. It has been so hard for most humans to comprehend, that the purpose of their coming forth is to create and the only mission is one for joy. That is the only reason you are here.

You knew then before your birth, that you would be guided through your every step toward your journey to your greatest desires. You knew that you can be, do or have anything that you desired, *effortlessly,* as you knew of the guidance you would receive.

As you came forth, it was designed that you would not remember your past lives. But remembering *who you really are* and *where you came from* before your birth, is something you must remember in order to know the purpose you came forth and most importantly to be aware of your guidance.

Can you see why so many people are not happy due to struggle and suffering? Doesn't it make sense that they must have lost themselves in this physical journey, that most do not know w*ho they really are*, where they came from, how powerful they are and their purpose for being here?

With this consciousness shift that is happening at this powerful time, can you understand why it is called the great awakening? It is the awakening to *who you really are, where you came from* and the *purpose you chose to come here.* Can you understand how everything is going to change once you receive the clarity and the awareness of how powerful you are, how worthy you are, how you can have, be or do anything you choose? And can you understand how much fun and happiness you will have, once you gain the awareness of your freedom, and the clarity that your only mission for being here is for the joy of it?

When you awaken to *who you really are*, then it shall be known and shown to you in your clarity, the truth of the purpose of your being here.

Knowing Where You Go After Physical Life

Now that you understand that you are *thought energy* living inside a physical body, which was the only way to enter into the physical realm, it is important for you to know that every single cell of your body is also made of thought energy.

Deep within the core of every cell is thinking energy. If not, your hand would not know how to be a hand, your fingers would not know how to be fingers, and your organs would not know how to be organs, not without thought energy to create their movement.

When you are in a state of stress, you are distressed and not *who you really are,* because who you are, is pure positive energy. You are powerful. Stress is a state of being in the illusions of fear and powerlessness. It is an indicator that you are not in your natural state. Your cells are also pure positive thinking energy and when they are in a state of stress defined as illness, they too are not being who they really are.

In order to be who you really are, you must feel good for your energy to rise to where you are from, which is where your natural powers are. When you are stressed, your energy vibrates in a very low frequency, but when you feel good, your energy reaches a high frequency vibrating level that is able to flow throughout the Universe. This powerful stream then reaches the location of where you come from, which is where your true powers are.

The term "bad" energy is wrongfully used. There is absolutely no source of bad energy. There is only one source of energy in the entire universe and it is of good pure positive energy. When you verbalize the words that you feel bad or that something has bad energy, there is no such thing. It is only because your energy is vibrating in a low frequency, which cannot reach the level to where you come from, which *is who you really are* and your emotions always indicate the level of your frequency. Your feelings will let you know what frequency you are vibrating on.

So, when you feel bad, it is to let you know that your frequency is too low. Feeling bad is that feeling of discord, and when your frequency is low, you are not *who you really are* due to not being able to reach your powers, which are at home where you come from.

The energy within the cells of your body also needs to connect to where they came from, for they too need to reach their powers in order to function properly. So as you feel stress, fear or any emotion that feels bad, you are stopping your cells from functioning. You are not allowing your cells to reach the frequency needed to function properly, and when your cells can't function they will become ill, for when you are not at ease, you are in dis-ease. In a prolonged state of stress or disease, they'll eventually stop functioning and deteriorate.

Now in order to raise your frequency, you must return to who you really are which is, your natural state of feeling good. When you are feeling good, you are allowing your cells to do what they need to do to remain healthy. The truth is, when you feel good, you can never be sick or ill, for it would defy the law of energy.

If a doctor were to stop prescribing medication to his patients, but would instead advise them to change their moods, he would hold the *key* to the awareness that he can naturally heal his patients.

All illnesses including cancer are all caused by oneself. By choosing to feel stress, fear, anger or anything that disconnects one from the stream of *who they really are;* they are refusing to allow their cells to do what they need in order to remain healthy.

Did you ever ask yourself why you need to sleep? Of course it's because you feel tired, but what do you think the real purpose for sleeping is? And why is it when you do not feel good, you naturally feel the need to sleep?

The only purpose of sleep is to release all the resistance you were holding on to, to let go of all fear, hatred and problems you think you may have. In the physical world, humans were designed with the need to sleep, because the purpose of sleep is to release all resistance or disparity.

When humans sleep, where do they go? When you sleep your body remains where it is, but the real you returns back home to where you're from, back to the purest of energy. In the non-physical world where you came from, there is no need for sleep, because there is no resistance due to its consistency of pure energy in its highest level. This realm you are from is where your powers are and you go back there to again reach the level of *who you really are,* and as you reawaken from your sleep state, you are again refreshed to your natural state of *who you really are.*

As you can see, the true purpose of sleep is very important and is in fact vital to your physical machine. If you didn't release your disparity, your cells would eventually deteriorate from the lack of not being able to function, due to not connecting to the powers that they have which gives them the remembering of their own functions. It is important to know, a physical body cannot survive in stress, as it will eventually stop functioning.

So when humans experiences death, where do they go? They do not die as most may think. The death experience is so close to the sleep experience, that one goes back to where they came from and reconnects to *who they really are.* The only difference between what you call death and a sleep state is, in the transition labeled as death, you do not place the game of your physical world on pause, but instead cancel the game to start over. After being so lost within the illusions of disparity, the physical body stops functioning and you opt for a fresh start to the life experience.

There is no difference between those who make their transition through cancer or illnesses, or those who make their transition through an accident or suicide. They are all created by default. Those who make their transition through physical illness are as discorded as those who make their transition through suicide. Someone who chooses suicide intentionally cancels the game and in most cases, the ones' who are labeled with physical illness, believe that they have no choice in the matter.

Humans have been programmed to believe that death is to be feared, that is why most fear it. There is no such thing as death. It is not something to fear. Do you fear your sleep state? Do you fear or feel despair when you take a nap or say goodnight before you enter your sleep state? Perhaps one should be joyful and wish them "bon voyage" on their trip back home.

Part Three

The Powers That You Hold

As you now have the awareness that you are powerful, you will want the clarity as to what your powers are. As you read Part Three, you shall hold the clarity of your natural powers, which most have over-looked throughout their journey, because most have been misled of their purpose and their true nature.

There is a truth beyond your existence in this physical time space reality, *a truth beyond what it really is.* These are powerful secrets that were meant to be kept from the public. Now, due to the great awakening, the people will be guided to the secrets that shall be revealed, from the remembering of the powers that they hold. These powerful secrets have been suppressed from the mass population of the human race, and from what you are about to read they shall be revealed to you. You will hold the key to master your powers, *if you allow it.*

The Power Of Emotion

Now that you are aware of the system of emotion, I shall explain it in more detail to clarify this powerful tool that you hold.

Emotion is one of the most powerful and sophisticated system, cleverly designed to perfection. It was designed for your guidance in the physical world and guides you to the path of your greatest desires. Everyone has one attached to them. Every single human on earth was born with this magnificent powerful system. I cannot emphasize enough the importance of your emotions.

Most humans have no clue of its importance or the true purpose for such a magnificent system, yet everyone operates from it every single day, minute and seconds throughout their existence in this physical realm. Many are condemned for the natural use of its powerful operation. It is one of the most important and powerful functions that humans hold. It was designed for your experience here.

In the non-physical world, you are thought energy and in this physical world, you are thought energy emotions. In the physical world, *thought energy* and *emotions* are all one. You cannot separate them and one cannot operate without the other. There are no exceptions for any humans on Earth.

An emotion is a feeling, something that you feel. Everything in every moment is functioning within the system of emotion, including all your physical senses. Emotion in itself is a sensor, the most powerful sensor within your physical senses. Your sense of touch is to feel what you are touching. Your hearing will trigger a feeling about what you are listening to. Your taste will trigger a feeling about the food you taste. Your sense of smell will trigger how you feel about an aroma. Your sense of sight will trigger how you feel from what you are looking at.

Your emotions are the most powerful of all senses. They are the masters of all your physical senses. Some may believe they can suppress their emotions, but that is impossible. Because when they think they have succeeded in doing so, they shall feel numb and the feeling of numbness is indeed a strong emotion and does not feel good. No matter how hard one tries to escape their own built-in system of emotion, one shall never succeed in doing so because emotions are part of *who they are* in this physical world.

Emotion is a *key* to the powers that you hold. Where most had no idea of this key and the secret of its powers, now more and more humans upon this planet hold the awareness of the truth beyond the purpose of emotions.

Now, what you have read about emotions does resonate with you, because it makes perfect sense. However, there is *a truth beyond what it really is* and a truth beyond its real purpose. The only purpose for your emotion is for your guidance in the physical world.

What if I told you, your emotions are an extension of the greater part of yourself which is in the non-physical world, and it's how the greater part of yourself communicates with you to guide you? What if I told you, your emotions are guiding you to your greatest desires? That's exactly what your emotions were designed to do for you in this physical world. It is the bigger part of yourself connecting with you and guiding you to the perfect path of everything you desire.

It is telling you the level of your frequency. Feeling good is your nature. When you are feeling good, your energy is vibrating at a frequency that is very high and that's why it feels good. When you feel bad, your frequency is low. Your emotions are telling you the level of the frequency you are operating on.

You knew before you came forth, you would be guided through the communication of your emotions. When you feel good, no matter for what reason, you are following the path to all that you desire, and you knew that when you did not feel good, it is only because you were off the track or on the wrong path to your desires. Your emotions are guiding your thoughts in every moment in response to what you are thinking. If you think a thought and you are aware of how you feel, it is your guidance communicating with you.

If one were to go within to feel their own being, and always listen to their own guidance, they would be living a life of growth, freedom and joy; *effortlessly* creating everything that they desire. However, most humans are programmed to believe, one must look outside of themselves into the society ruled by man to search for their paths as they are left only to question, why life is not working out for them. It is an absolute promise to you, if one is not aware of their own guidance to the path of freedom, they shall be led to the path of others' control. No exception to that, for anyone.

Once you hold the awareness that your path is given to you and you start looking within to *who you really are*, it is an absolute promise to you that you will be guided to everything that you want. You will be guided to everything that you came forth to be, to do, to have, and you shall live a life of growth, freedom, and joy, which is the only reason you intended to come forth into this physical experience.

There is nothing more important in the entire Universe than for you to feel good. Feeling good is the path to your desires. Resistance, fear, anger and everything that feels bad is not recognized or felt back home by your greater self, because in the non-physical world which you came from, you are pure positive energy. Pure positive energy is the only source of energy in all existence.

Before you came into this physical realm, you knew of the illusions of disparity you may face, and the importance of being guided to your right path. You knew that there is no limit to what you desire. You knew what you wanted and exactly what would bring you joy, and what you wanted would change, which the nature of change would lead you to evolve into an even greater being. You knew you had the freedom to change what you wanted, knowing it would be even better than the visions you had before you came forth.

You knew that the physical world was in perfect balance and harmony, governed by Universal laws. You knew that everything you needed would be provided for you. You knew that your purpose for coming forth was to create and your only mission was for joy. You knew that you would never be alone that you will always be guided, that you would be safely guided through every step of your physical journey.

The most important thing that you knew before you came forth into this physical realm is, if you were at any moment to forget where you came from or to forget *who you really are,* your *emotional guiding system* would remind you. Can you understand how eager you were to come forth into this physical world?

Now imagine yourself back home in the non-physical world before you came forth. See this. Imagine it. Hold a picture of it.

Imagine yourself as a big ball of white energy. You are eager to come forth and say to yourself:

"I will remain here in the non-physical realm and send a small part of this energy that I Am into the physical realm .I will guide myself, as the smaller part of myself goes forth into the physical dimension.

As a part of myself goes forth into the physical world, I shall communicate with myself with every emotion that I feel. I shall feel my path as my energy vibrates at a high frequency, and if I disconnect from my path and loose myself within the illusions of the physical world, I shall feel the discord within myself. So as I feel good for no matter what reason, I shall know that I Am following my bliss and I will be on the right path toward my desires, which I chose to come forth to create and enjoy."

So, a small part of yourself came forth in awareness that you shall always be guided to the path of your greatest desires through the emotions that you feel. It is like having an invisible extension cord connected to the bigger part of yourself. You feel these emotions inside your body, because *who you really are* is within your physical body. The energy that you feel is who you really are.

When you feel good, you are creating with your thoughts the frequency needed to reach the bigger part of yourself which remains in the non-physical world. When you feel bad, it is only because your frequency is too low due to the thoughts you are thinking and you cannot connect with *who you really are.* You feel the dis-cord (the disconnection of the extension cord) when you feel bad. When you feel good, you feel your connection. That is why a joyful and happy person shall live longer in the physical world than someone who is stressed or discorded. As you feel bad, you are disallowing the energy within your cells to connect with *who they are.* They must be connected in order to remember their functions.

In the rule of man, you were programmed to believe that you must search outside of yourself and look to the rules of society to find your path. The rule-makers knew that when you know *who you really are* you can no longer be under the control of others. That is the absolute truth. There is nothing more important than for you to *feel good,* because when you feel good, you are not alone, you are always safe and nothing can bring you harm because you are connected to your higher power.

When you feel good, no matter how bad your environment or condition may seem to be, everything must change. It is law. Most will try with great effort to take physical action to change a situation in order to feel good, but the secret is, if you feel good no matter what the situation is, the situation must change, with no effort on your part. It has to, because that's how your energy that creates worlds operates within this physical world. That's how powerful you are. If you don't feel good, you are being guided to stop looking at what you are looking at, stop doing what you are doing and most importantly stop thinking or focusing on what you are thinking or focused upon.

If you are feeling good, keep doing what you are doing. It is as simple as that. Always being aware of how you feel and most importantly, following your guidance is the *secret* and *most powerful key.*

The Power Of Thought

What if I told you that everything around you is an illusion? All that you see, the chair you sit on, the street you walk on, the stores that you see, the inside of your home, outside, cars, your clothes, your bed, trees, the animals and every single person is in form of *thought energy*. Whether you believe this or not, it is true. Everything that you think is solid, is not. Every single thing that you see in every moment consists of *thought energy*.

If you were to see deep within the core of every physical object, you would see powerful moving energy, because everything that you see, including yourself, is made from *thought energy*. You are energy of pure love and joy; it is the natural energy of *which you really are*. You are energy of feeling and when you feel good, you feel *who you really are*. You can't see yourself, you can only feel yourself because you are energy.

In the non-physical world, you are *thought energy* and all you do is create, create and create and you are creating through thought. Your thought visions are real, but not in physical form. In order to come forth, you had to create yourself, create a *thought vision* of yourself. You came forth into the body of a baby and in the physical world you keep creating yourself in every moment. Your body, the trees, everything was a vision in thought. Since you are energy of love, joy and well-being it was the perfect vision, a perfect creation. You held a vision for everything from the mountains, the trees, to all the beings you wanted to meet throughout your journey in your physical world.

When you came forth within the physical realm, you did not physically travel to get here. Your energy did not come as a stream of white light. You did not travel through time and space. You traveled through thought, you visualized yourself here. You are not here at this moment. You are only focused in thought of being here. You are here in your visions of yourself being here. You are thought energy and you will always be thought energy. You will never be human; you are only operating in thought within the human body.

You are still back home but in a vision of yourself being here, and time is an illusion which you shall understand as you read further. You are still in the non-physical world which is your home and in a moving image in thought of yourself being here.

Part Four

The Dreams Within Your Sleep State

When you go to sleep at night, you release yourself from your thoughts and visions of being in the physical realm and you are back to your original state of non-physical and pure energy, which is what your reality is when you're back home to _who you really are_. Back home you know, that you always exist in the now. You know you have not been gone for years; you are always in the now within your focused thoughts in visions of being in the physical dimension. The physical world is not reality but only a thought that is projecting within your _thought energy_ in the non-physical world.

What you are about to read will create greater clarity within you.

What you think is real, in this moment, it is not. When you go to sleep, you believe your sleep state is not real, but it's the opposite of that. When you sleep you are back home to _who you really are_. Your world here is only a dream or a thought that you are focused on. The only difference is that in the non-physical world you are aware of your visions of being here, in the non-physical world you do not sleep.

So one might ask "If when I'm sleeping is where I'm from and who I really am, if I remember a bad dream or nightmare, does it mean that back home is a bad place?" It is not a bad place at all. It is all pure positive energy. Your dreams are only a communication to you that you are either on the right or wrong track to the path of your physical creations. They are telling you whether you are creating toward what you desire or creating the unwanted within your physical world.

Bad dreams are just telling you, you must change the way you think and feel because you are mis-creating, and you can change your creations in your physical world by changing how you think and feel. For example, if you focus your thinking on negative thoughts for a prolonged period of time, you will eventually have a negative dream in your sleep state. The reason you have a bad dream is to bring to your awareness, what you were most focused upon in your physical state, was not leading you to your path of your true desires. It is only yourself coming to realization that you must focus your thinking with positive thoughts.

The important thing to notice is how you felt in your dream state. The pictures or movie that you think you see is just a picture or projection that was placed there for your understanding. It communicates with you, telling you what emotion you were operating on in the physical world.

When you feel good in your dreams, it is a message telling you that how you think and feel in the physical world is on the right path to your desires. You are in the physical reality for the fun of being here and to create, and when you begin loosing track of yourself in this fabulous game, you must go back home to remember the rules of the game.

So what you are dreaming in your sleep state is a message telling you what you are in the process of creating in the physical realm. Now, the pictures or movie that you saw in your dream may not come to manifest themselves, but the way you felt in your dream is in the process of manifesting itself. If you have a bad dream, be thankful for the communication you received and start changing the way you've been thinking and feeling, and focus on the opposite of it to create what you really want.

When you feel tired or sleepy, it is a natural calling for you to place your game on pause and go back to your real state of being, to refresh yourself. When you are tired, you are being called to go back home and when you sleep, it is to remember the rules of the game of the physical world.

It is the same for those who feel stressed. They feel tired and have a natural need to sleep more than someone who is happy. More evidence of this, is shown when someone is sick or ill, they will feel a greater need to sleep because they are being called in a more powerful way to place the game on pause and to go back home to refresh themselves. They are being called to the awareness that their sickness is not real, that it is not who they really are and not what they intended to come forth to be. Sickness is only an illusion that has been fabricated through ones' own thought.

Your Existence Expanding The Universe

Thought Energy is who you are and you are living within your visions of being here, you can't help but to create. As you focus your thoughts on yourself being in the physical world, you are still a creator within your thoughts. You are creating, not with action from your body like most are programmed to believe, but with your vision of thought. Once you reach that awareness and clarity, you will know that you have the power to control *your* world, to easily create *your* world the way you want it to be, to create the reality that you desire through your very own thoughts.

Before you came forth into the physical realm, it was clear to you that you came here to create your own reality and not the realities of others. Everyone is creating their own world and if you try to create other people's worlds or realities for them, you shall lose your path and stray from the purpose for being here and you shall lose yourself in others' realities.

Everyone is in their own state to create their own world. For you to try to fix anyone, is defying Universal laws, but to inspire others to know *who they really are,* is to be in harmony with Universal laws.

Now that you hold an awareness of the nature of *who you really are*, a natural creator through thought, you will be aware that you are creating everything that surrounds you.

Again, apply your imagination and place this picture within your mind:

Once again, see yourself back home as a large ball of white energy. This is your thinking energy. So, a small spec of your energy came forth, as the larger part of yourself decided to stay in the non-physical world to guide yourself in your physical world. Now, another spec of that same energy also came forth, and another which are defined as every single human upon earth. You are all part of that same thought energy. You are all *one*, and everything that surrounds you is also part of that same energy.

Everyone is part of the same energy. When you decided to come forth, you knew then that you would become individual creators within the physical world. You are all the same thought energy but you came forth to expand creation in different perspectives. You are all part of one consciousness in the non-physical world, but as you came forth in the physical world, you multiplied your consciousness as individual creators through different perspectives operating through different physical bodies.

As you are here, you are expanding thought. You are multiplying thought for your non-physical world. So as you are here in the physical dimension, you are expanding your consciousness energy; meaning, you are expanding the Universal thought energy.

Your being here is expanding the Universe. Do you understand your worthiness and the magnificence of your being here? Are you aware of the powerful being that you are? That your being here is expanding the entire Universe? You are creating in your physical world which is your purpose for coming forth. Therefore, you are expanding the Universe.

Here is the bigger picture: All that you are and all that is, is 100% pure positive thought energy that creates. You are a creator. The Universe is creation. You *are* the Universe, the Universe that is creating.

Infinite Earths And Infinite Realities

What if I told you that there is not only one planet Earth, but as many Earths as there are people on its planet? And all these Earths exist in harmony with each other but in different realities? This is the absolute truth.

Every single person at present is creating a different version of the reality they desire in the physical world, which I shall call a movie.

We are all creating a different movie in our thoughts. Everyone is holding a different picture of their lives here and everyone is living in their own reality, according to their own perspective. There is not only one planet earth, but as many earths as there are humans.

Most humans were programmed to believe that they are all in one same reality within the physical world. You are not. When two humans are together, they are operating within the same energy but in different realities. So let's say that two different beings are standing next to each other looking in the same direction, one can see a tree or a certain object and the other person can be seeing a totally different object.

I'd like to tell you a little story which I've told many. This story is a great example that humans are living in different realities.

For a time, I would walk along the same street as I went about my business each day. It was a beautiful street. Everything always seemed so green. It was a quiet street in a suburban upper middle class area and I would often notice luxury vehicles and beautiful homes. The environment was friendly and everyone would smile and seemed happy. I loved walking on that street.

Further up the road was an intersection and before I would pass it each day there was the most beautiful tree. It was a magnolia tree with huge flowers which had a beautiful aroma. Every morning I was excited to walk by that tree.

One day as I was walking along the street, I noticed someone. When the lady introduced herself, I discovered she was my neighbor. She began visiting me at my home where we would share a cup of coffee over conversation, and as we became friends she would tell me all of her past experiences throughout her life's journey.

I was not aware then as I am now, upon the reflection that she, very often, spoke in a negative manner.

One day she came for a visit and she was more negative than usual. The complaints about her life were extreme. I thought I needed to help her feel better, as most of us would; thinking we can fix someone. Attempting to make her feel better, I told her about the beautiful tree that was on that lovely street we both walked on every day.

I told her to look at the tree and feel how beautiful it was. I described the beautiful aroma of its flowers.

She told me that she had never seen that tree before, and that the only thing she saw every morning on the same spot I had described the tree to be, was a big old smelly garbage bin. She complained about how tired she was of smelling its bad odor everyday as she walked by that spot. I told her, I had never seen a garbage bin there but only the magnolia tree.

After our coffee that day as she left, my attempts for uplifting her were unsuccessful, and I was left feeling in a low mood myself.

The next morning, I was on my regular walk up the same street and I remembered my neighbor telling me about the garbage bin. So I decided to pay attention expecting to see a garbage bin where the magnolia tree was, to see if she was right.

To my surprise, she was right. Below my beautiful tree, I saw a very dirty garbage bin. I noticed the unpleasant smell and I was puzzled as to why I had never noticed that bin before.

So as time went by, she continued visiting me and telling me about her life experiences which I did not want to hear, but out of politeness and not wanting to be rude, as most humans do, I would listen to her stories even though I did not feel good hearing them.

One day she told me that a robbery took place in the area. Another day she talked about someone who was attacked. And another day she told me about her friend whose vehicle was vandalized.

I was surprised to hear this. I always saw the area as a beautiful and safe place to live. As time went on I started hearing more and more sirens at night, from police cars to ambulances to fire trucks. The beautiful area I was living in, I came to realize, was not the safest place to live.

As I kept taking my morning walks, I started seeing more and more people on the street asking for money. I began noticing the beautiful homes that I had always seen were now separated by small buildings in between that operated as food banks and walk-in clinics, one in particular having a very long line.

Instead of the vehicles in the area that were once looking new to me, I noticed that most of the vehicles that past by me were older vehicles, one having a noisy muffler dragging on the street.

I had then come to realize, that the area was not so beautiful after all. I was then feeling unhappy and unsafe.

That story was a great example that we all live in different worlds.

Now, what had happened to me was this. At the beginning of the story I was creating my own reality, according to what I desired. I was living in joy and I was surrounded by beauty. As I was focusing on my neighbor's experiences, I stopped creating my own reality and was entering her reality, seeing the world as she experienced it.

That garbage bin was always there, the reason I never saw it prior to meeting my neighbor was because it was invisible to me, but because my thought energy started focusing on her frequency, my frequency changed and I began operating under the same frequency that she was on, showing me evidence of her experiences. By trying to fix her reality, I became a part of it, instead of continuing to create my own.

Your Magnetic Field In Response To Your Frequency

I shall now bring you better clarity as to how the natural creation process operates in every human being within the physical world.

What if I told you that you are able to make something appear or disappear and you were able to place a picture in your thought and turn it into its physical object form? Whether you believe this or not, it is true.

In the story of the neighbor I encountered, I should point out that she was not at all to blame for my experience. When she first introduced herself, I felt a discord within me which was my emotional guidance system communicating to me that being around her was contrary to what I desired, but I did not listen and follow my own guidance.

When you don't listen to your guidance, you may very well be going on the wrong path without being aware of it and losing yourself in others realities. Everything that exists is part of the same energy.

In your physical world, you have The Law of Gravity. Gravity is also energy, it is a movement to keep physical objects grounded. Because you are thought energy in nature, you harmonize with gravity because gravity is energy. Now, the Law of Gravity is always in every moment operating. It will never stop operating for anyone. If it did, physical objects would start floating into space. It is a very sophisticated system and operates in perfection.

You are also *magnetic thought energy*. You are operating as a magnetic field in a perfection that never stops operating. In the physical world, you are by nature, *emotion magnetic thought energy*.

Just as gravity holds us on the surface of Earth in this physical realm, as a rule we are all surrounded by a magnetic field and our energy has a magnetic force. One could describe themselves as a magnet. As you are creating your world around you, your thought energy with its magnetic force is attracting other beings to you within your world. The nature of your thought energy is magnetic and this force is for the purpose of your own creations.

There is also an extremely important thing you need to remember. It is a Universal law that two different frequency levels cannot co-exist together. It is impossible. If they did, it would defy laws of energy, the Laws of the Universe.

When you feel good, you are operating in high frequency, but when you feel bad, you are operating in low frequency. The law is, two different frequencies cannot co-exist together. Therefore, when you feel good, you cannot feel bad at the same time, because they are two different frequencies.

So when I encountered my neighbor, I was being guided by my emotions from the very first moment. It is important to understand, I was not being warned that she was a bad person. Every single person is of pure energy in nature. My emotion was telling me what frequency I was operating on. It was guiding me in response to my own frequency. My emotion was responding to my own creation.

My neighbor was not at all to blame for my experience. What I didn't mention in the story is that earlier that same morning before I first noticed my neighbor walking on the same street, I did something that most humans would think of being an intelligent thing to do. I received knowledge on the false premise of the programmed belief that one must face reality. Before I met my neighbor that same morning, my cable TV was connected and the first thing I did was watch the news.

My thoughts were focused on a story of crime and violence, and even though I did not feel good about the story, I kept focusing on it. After watching that horrible news, which I was being guided by my emotions not to watch it due to it being opposite to the life I wanted, shortly after, I went for a walk and there I saw my neighbor for the first time. I wasn't aware that she was also in that same frequency.

If my neighbor was not to blame for my experience, was it the news that I was watching that morning? The news was not at all to blame for my experience.

There is another important *key* that I've yet to mention about the story. Before I started watching the news that morning, I awakened from my sleep in not the best of moods. I was complaining to myself about the weather and I was not grateful for anything which mean, I was being ungrateful for things in general.

I alone was responsible for my own experience, not my neighbor, not the news, not the weather. You see, when I woke up that morning, I did not pay attention to the way I was feeling. I was not aware of my own guidance, which is the path to my greatest desires. I was being guided by my higher self through my emotions that I was operating in a frequency which was contrary to what I desired. I was being firmly told by the way I felt that my frequency was operating in too low of a level.

My higher self was communicating with me to change my frequency. It was telling me that I was getting off track to *who I really am* which is happiness and joy, the same frequency as my desires. Every moment through our journey, our path to our greatest desires is shown to us but most humans don't listen to their path. That morning I was not aware of how I felt so of course, I was not aware that I was taking the wrong path. That morning if I would have been *aware* of the way I was feeling and if I could have immediately changed my thoughts to better feeling thoughts, my life experience at that time would have been different. I would have been creating a different reality. A reality of what I desired.

That morning the thought energy that I was operating on was in low frequency and because my thought energy is also a magnetic field, I was a magnet pulling to myself everything that was in the same frequency that I was on.

The famous quote you all heard "opposites attracts" is false knowledge. Do not bring that belief into your journey for it shall lead to confusion. Opposites do not attract. Someone cannot attract the opposite frequency that they are on.

If someone is in low bad feeling frequency, they cannot attract to themselves someone in high good feeling frequency. It cannot be it would defy Universal law. It is a law, that as a magnet you shall attract to you the people, the environment, the objects, the experiences and the thoughts which are in perfect harmony to your own frequency. So you see, if you think bad thoughts, you feel bad and you will attract bad things to yourself. But when you feel good you attract the good to yourself. It is Law and it shall be.

That morning I woke up thinking in low frequency. Without my awareness, I attracted to myself the news event which was my matching frequency and I attracted to myself my neighbor who was matching the same frequency. All these things added to the magnetic force of that frequency of miscreation, making it bigger and stronger. That is why the better it gets, the better it will get and the worse it gets, the worse it will get.

You must always be aware of how you feel. If you are not feeling good, you must come to the awareness of how you feel immediately and change your thoughts to better feeling thoughts and keep focusing on better thoughts until your emotions kick in to tell you that you are on the right track again.

You are a creator and your thought energy is the energy that creates worlds. Always be aware of how you feel. Your emotions are the most sophisticated and powerful system that you hold for your path towards your greatest desires. Your emotions do not create your reality. Your thoughts create your reality which is the vibrating energy that creates form. Your emotions are only guiding you to what you are creating with your thoughts.

Managing Your Own Frequency

The Universal laws are in perfect harmony with all creations and these Universal laws operate in the non-physical world exactly the same as in the physical world. When you eventually become truly aware that the physical world you are living in is in perfect harmony, you shall experience great freedom.

When you came forth to the physical world, you did not come forth to struggle or suffer. You did not come forth for lessons to be learned. The Universal laws never said that if you don't abide by its laws then you shall suffer. You are not being punished by a greater force outside of yourself, as some religions may program many to believe.

You are thought energy and creating is your nature. Therefore, you are *The Creator.* There are absolutely no forces separate from you that are more powerful.

You are the Power. You are the Universe. You are The Creator. You are the power that came forth to expand yourself in creation. As you are creating to expand yourself, the Universe is expanding because you are the Universe.

You came forth for the fun, excitement, pleasure, joy and freedom to create anything you desire. The world you are in is your own world. It is not the world of anyone else. It is your world that you are creating and others are creating their own worlds.

Nothing can harm you in your own world because you have the power to create it in whichever way you chose.

Every single person is creating their own world and their own reality, but all the different worlds operate within the same energy; therefore, the different realities are in harmony with each other. Everything in your own world is for the purpose of your own creation.

For example, a real estate agent is creating his own world and his magnetic field is attracting to him what he needs to create his world. Therefore, the magnetic field of his energy shall bring him what he needs for creating, which are the buyers.

Now you are creating your world and you want to purchase a home. Your energy field will attract the real estate agent for your own creation.

Every human that you meet is for the purpose of your own creation, to create your own reality. When you meet humans that are not so nice to you, it's because you've attracted them to yourself, also for the purpose of your own creation as they are your greatest teachers. They are reflecting to you your own level of frequency to let you know you are on the wrong path. But you must not trap yourself within their world and you must not try to fix them. It is not your job to make them feel better. That is the work of the Universe.

The creation of another's reality is absolutely none of your or anyone else's business. If you try and make it your business, you shall lose your path in creating your own reality. Look at it in this way. Everyone is being guided by their own natural powerful force of the Universe. Therefore, if the most powerful force of all, which is the force of the Universe, can't get through to them, how can a human possibly get through to them?

Infinite Intelligence: The Origin Of Thought

There is another power that which you hold, a secret that was meant to be kept amongst a few. Throughout history, the ones' who knew of this secret and applied it were labeled as the great master minds.

As you came forth into the physical world, you came forth not remembering your past lives for good reason. If you were to remember your past lives you would be focused in the past and this would prevent you from creating new realities, meaning your creative nature would cease. So you came forth not remembering your past lives but as you read previously, you have been here thousands of times. You never cease to exist.

In your non-physical world you remember all your past lives, but in the non-physical world there is no past or future, everything is in the now. The system of time does not exist there. You remember all of your past lives and know everything about all that was ever created in past lives and worlds. In your non-physical state, you have access to massive infinite amounts of information.

Because you are infinite in nature, who you really are in the non-physical world, is thought energy. You can also be defined as genius or infinite intelligence. As a small part of yourself is presently focused in the physical world with no recollection of your past lives, the bigger part of yourself that remained in the non-physical reality has access to all the information from your past lives and everything that ever existed.

In your non-physical state, you know that your physical body is not who you really are and the same goes for your physical brain. Your physical brain is but a part of your physical body. The physical brain does not create thoughts and your physical brain is not the source of your intelligence. The physical brain only functions as a transmitter and receiver. It is a receiver and transmitter of information. It receives information and sends out information. Your physical brain does not create thoughts, it only receives thoughts.

You are connected to the bigger part of yourself (which is you) in your non-physical world and that bigger part of yourself consists of infinite intelligence therefore, all thoughts that you have come from your own infinite intelligence. They are received by you from your higher power.

In your physical world as you are now focused, you have easy access to any information that you need from your infinite intelligence. Due to the Universal laws and your magnetic nature, your infinite intelligence will always send you thoughts that match your frequency level.

However, most have forgotten *who they really are* and have lost their path somewhere along their physical journey. They have forgotten the power that they hold to easily and naturally access their own infinite intelligence. Once you hold the awareness of *who you really are* you will know that you are a *powerful intelligent creative genius*. There is absolutely no exception to that for any human upon this planet. It is law.

The Universal Laws In Perfect Harmony

The Universal laws (law of energy) are governing and operating from the non-physical dimension which is the head office where all creations begin to take place. Because the physical realm is an extension of the non-physical realm, the exact same Universal laws are functioning through your focused thoughts within your physical world.

Now as I've already mentioned, in the non-physical reality you are thought energy at its purest level. You are love energy, appreciation energy, and joy energy, meaning that you are always pure positive energy which is always vibrating at its natural high frequency level. Low frequency energy does not exist in the non-physical realm.

Because of the Universal laws, which are revolving around high frequency, when you came forth still operating by these laws, the low frequencies in the physical world are not recognized by your true self in the non-physical realm. In the non-physical realm, low frequency energy is not recognized as a bad thing. Therefore, it will give you whatever you create in that same frequency. Being pure positive in nature, the larger part of yourself, believes that you are always creating what you want. You are so loved that it gives you everything that you are creating with your thoughts.

Before you came forth you knew exactly how the creation process worked because you are, at every Universal level, a creator. There is absolutely no right or wrong, no good or bad in the energy that creates worlds, which is what *you are*. The Universal laws do not judge anything as good or bad because they naturally operate in 100% pure positive energy. What you define as good or bad the Universe only reads it as good.

Do you understand how loved you are by the Universe? The Universe will always yield to you. You have the freedom to create anything you want.

The Universe doesn't hear you when you say "I don't want that thing". It only reads frequencies and presents the perfect match to your creation. The Universal laws and its forces yield to you anything you create. ***That's how loved you are.***

You create anything that you want with your thoughts. ***That's how powerful you are.*** You can create anything that you want and there is never anything wrong with your creation through the eyes of the Universe. ***That's how much freedom you have.*** And on top of that you came forth with a powerful guiding system that will guide your path through every thought that you think. ***That's how fortunate you are.***

Part Five

The Secret To Purposely Creating What You Want

The System Of Time

Time is an illusion. In the non-physical world time does not exist. Most believe that time is for the purpose of having a regimented schedule: to keep ones' life in order, to get up at a certain time, to eat at a certain time, to sleep at a certain time, to make it to work at a certain time or to meet someone at a certain time. But there is another reason, another very important purpose as to why the physical world is a time space reality.

As you are a natural creator, the true purpose for time is for the molding of your creations through your thoughts. If time didn't exist, the images that you would hold in your thoughts would manifest or appear immediately in your reality.

Imagine if what you desired most would appear instantly, in return what you did not desire would also have to appear instantly. For example, you vision the beautiful home that you want and like magic you receive it that same day, but at the same time, you hold a vision of fear of it burning down. Well, your great desire would also be gone as fast as you receive it.

However, there are those who have become such powerful deliberate creators through mastering the key of the awareness and clarity of *who they really are* and have the ability to manifest almost instantaneously. These are the great master minds.

But before you want to achieve that level, you want to be prepared to create exactly what you desire.

Many hold a very strong desire they consider very big according to their beliefs and become frustrated or disappointed when they haven't received what they are asking for. First, the art has to be *mastered*. You would have to practice and focus on being *who you really are* at all times, no matter what.

You see, the system of time is for the purpose of perfecting your creations. Deliberate creation is an art in itself. As for everything else, you do create something in your existence every single day. Little parts of the movie you pictured in your thoughts do manifest in every moment.

The only purpose of this magnificent system of time is to mold your thoughts for the creation of your desired reality. If you desire a home you need to be specific in the details. Add the stairs you want, the rooms you want and all the other details.

Now let's say that you are now purchasing a home and you believe it to be your dream home. So you move in and notice that the roof is leaking. Somewhere along your creation you had mixed thoughts as to whether or not something would go wrong with your new home. You see, you must continue to the perfection of your home in your thoughts. This would be a perfect example that you must know what you do not want in order to know what you do want. In this case you would now naturally desire a house with a good roof.

Your thoughts keep creating in every moment of your life and time is for the purpose of creation.

Desire Is Your Nature

Some were programmed to believe that having desires is wrong, which is especially common in some religious teachings. That in itself is a false belief. Desire is the first natural step to creation. One must desire something in order to create it and since creation is the nature of your existence, to desire is also the nature of who you are.

In the non-physical world you had a strong *desire* to come forth into the physical world. To hold a belief against having desires, the fact that someone holds a desire, not to desire is indeed a desire in itself. Do you see the confusion this creates?

In order to create something that you want, you must first have a desire for it. Desire comes naturally as it is part of your creative nature, and as you hold a desire for something, you will automatically begin to receive a vision of it.

To purposely create something you desire, you must hold a pure thought of it. As you are a magnet in nature, your infinite intelligence will deliver to you more thoughts that match the same frequency that you are operating on. If your frequency is operating at a high level, which is your natural state of feeling good, your infinite intelligence will deliver to you all the answers required toward your desire. Never doubt the Universal forces.

If you are not sure what level your frequency is on, pay attention to your emotions as they are always the best indicators. Your emotion is the only indicator of your frequency level and it is the only purpose that you have emotions. Always be aware of your guidance. If you are not feeling good, change your thought to a better feeling thought. You are creating what you are thinking and your emotions are telling you what you are creating.

Feel Your Way To Your Desire

The energy that creates worlds operates within a natural system of creation. It operates effortlessly within a specific triad: *The Triad of Creation.* A brief overview of this powerful triad, used to purposely create what you desire, is as follows:

The first step is to desire something and have a pure thought vision of your desire.

The second step is to feel your desire. This step is very important and it will happen naturally as you continue to focus on your pure thought vision.

When you first begin focusing on your desire it will just be a vision, a picture or thought and your infinite intelligence will transmit additional thoughts and answers to match your desire. Now, your emotions are the powerful key. Keep on your vision and then your emotions are going to start powering up your engine for your magnetic field to begin the attraction. This is when the natural high frequency feeling will begin to accumulate within you. Your desires will start to feel real. Once you start feeling what it's like to be in the vision of your desire, it will naturally and effortlessly begin feeling as though you are really there when you think about it. This is a sign that your desire is in the beginning process of manifesting itself into its physical form.

At this stage, it's important that you remain in a good feeling place. Now is the time to intentionally and purposely maintain good feeling thoughts. Feel good for any reason. And if you don't feel good try to change the way you feel by changing any thoughts that you are thinking as fast as you possibly can. Go smell the flowers. Go for a walk in the park. Do anything that you can to keep you focused in a good feeling place. It is of great importance that you try to keep your frequency at a high level at this point to manifest your desire.

The Compartments Within Your Belief System

Step one is to desire something and to hold a pure thought vision of what you desire.

Step two is to let the feeling of your desire naturally flow through you, and to stay in a good feeling place.

The third step is to believe your desire. *The power of belief* is the most important element to create what you desire. Most may think that this is the hard part but in fact it is the easiest part of all.

If you have practiced the first and second steps, the belief shall come naturally to you and you will feel it in a powerful way. Your belief will transmit a signal to the Universe. It confirms to the Universe that you are ready to receive the creation in its physical form.

The power of belief is a powerful system in itself. If you are not aware of how your belief system operates, it will kick in on its own and produce not only wanted beliefs but also unwanted beliefs without your awareness of it.

What exactly is a belief? A belief is a thought that you keep focusing on. As you focus or think about something in a prolonged timing, it will naturally and effortlessly turn into a belief, a system that functions on its own.

The system of belief consists of two compartments. Use your imagination and picture this:

Think of your mind as a circle. Inside this circle there are two boxes which represent the two different compartments within your belief system. One compartment is called the **doubt-box**. The second compartment is called the **self-box**.

The *doubt-box* contains all the beliefs from other people's beliefs and opinions, and all the beliefs that were programmed in you by society. Those beliefs are very strong because they are all the beliefs you picked up along your journey in the physical world. This includes lessons that were taught in schools, churches, the controlled societies and the people that surrounded you. Most are not aware that they are operating from beliefs that are inside their doubt-box, the beliefs created from others' beliefs, realities and opinions.

The *self-box* contains all the beliefs that are naturally created from the great awakening of *who you really are* and the powers you hold. It contains all the beliefs of great freedom, beliefs that anything is possible, that you are powerful and are pure positive energy. It contains the beliefs of everything you knew before you came forth into the illusions of the physical realm.

Most have been operating from their *doubt-box* throughout their physical journey and therefore, it has become the bigger compartment within their belief system.

If the System of Time did not exist, you would never be able to change your beliefs. When you desire something, what may often happen is your doubt-box will hold onto others' beliefs that your desire is not possible. This is another reason why one must be grateful for the system of time, to fill in their *self-box* so it can overpower their doubt-box.

The largest false belief that is contained in most people's doubt-box is that *one must face reality*. When people tell you to "face reality" what they are really telling you is to face other people's realities. This is the "reality" of the controlled society.

Once you begin to *purposely* create what you desire, you are in the process of filling in your powerful *self-box*. When you begin to purposely create what you desire, your doubt-box may contradict your self-box because, in many cases, ones' doubt-box is the most dominant box. It will contradict your desires due to its own beliefs that it cannot happen, that it is not real and you must face reality, that your desire is too big and that you are not deserving of it. Most are programmed by the false belief that ones' great desires can only be created through hard physical work. That is one of the greatest lies placed upon the human race.

Now, if you have a vision of your desire and your doubt-box kicks in, you must cancel out what it tells you by saying *"That was an old belief. I have the power to create anything I desire."* You must keep repeating that as many times as possible. Every time the thought of powerlessness is felt, you must say: *"That was an old belief. I have the power to create anything I desire."*

A belief is only a thought that you are focused on for a prolonged period of time, so as you keep telling your self-box that you have a new belief, eventually your self-box will overpower the doubt-box with its new belief.

This is yet another reason to be grateful for the system of time. It allows you to fill your self-box till it becomes the most powerful compartment in your system of belief. Time is on your side working in full force to mold your thoughts into your belief system, allowing you to create what you desire.

The System Of Belief: Your Natural Transmitter

In your non-physical world you are a powerful creative genius. The thoughts you focused on became a reality within your visions immediately because you are an expert in the creation process. It is naturally who you are and as time does not exist in the non-physical dimension, everything is created in the now.

So you see, as soon as you have a desire and hold the vision of it in thought, you have already created it. It already exists, but not in physical form. The Universe, which is *who you really are,* does not know the difference between what you hold in your thought or something that you are observing in physical form. The Universe truly does not know the difference. So what you think, is just a thought, the Universe thinks it's something that already exists in your experience, and continues to create based on that thought. It is real but invisible to the human eye, but it has been created and with your powers you shall naturally transform it into its physical form.

Here is an example of dollars because dollars are what many desire:

For some reason, you would like $10,000. Now sit in your chair, close your eyes and visualize that there is $10,000 at your feet on the floor in front of you. Now it is done. You have created $10,000 and as you open your eyes the dollars are there. This is how powerful you *really* are, but at the present time, where you are now, most who would open their eyes the dollars would not be there.

The dollars have been created, but the reason that most wouldn't see the dollars is because the dollars are in the invisible realm and they will remain in the invisible realm until your belief system, your self-box, holds the belief that the dollars are there. The dollars did not appear because you did not believe. The doubt-box was overpowering your self-box. That's the power of belief.

The doubt-box has been functioning at a strong level for most of your life, while your self-box has been relatively inactive. You cannot destroy your doubt-box but once you know *who you really are* and how *powerful you really are* your self-box will start filling up very fast and become more powerful than your doubt-box. As you are reading this book you are filling up your self-box in a powerful way.

The only reason the dollars were not at your feet is because you did not believe. But if you look at your feet and you do truly believe that there is $10,000, it shall be there in its physical form. It is law. The Universal laws say that it must be.

Your belief is a powerful signal transmitting the confirmation to the Universe that you are ready for what you asked for in its physical form. It does not matter if your belief is what you consider as a wrong belief or a right belief, a good belief or a bad belief. A belief is a belief and your belief is transmitted to the Laws of the Universe as a firm decision for it to be.

But thanks to the fabulous existence of time, you have the ability to change your beliefs. You cannot destroy your beliefs, you can only change them. It is the same for creation. It cannot be destroyed, it can only be changed.

As you become aware of the powerful being that you really are, your self-box will be operating in full force and eventually you'll come to the awareness that the only purpose you desire something is because you believe you will feel better in having it. Feeling good is the nature of *who you really are*.

As you carefully ponder and focus on the messages that you have read, you shall hold the key to the powers of becoming, doing and having anything you desire *naturally and effortlessly*.

The Triad Of Creation: The 90 Day Process

Here is the formula to purposely create what you desire:

In order for this process to be affective, you must turn off your television for 90 days. Yes, that's correct. Turn off that programming tube for 90 days.

For some, this may be the most difficult part of the process. Deciding to follow through, will all depend on how much you want change.

If you must be around others, be around those who are positive and try to avoid negative people for the duration of the 90 day process. It will not be a surprise to you that after 90 days, your desire of being around positive environments and surroundings shall become habitual to you.

It will take 90 days to create anything you desire for this is the time required to naturally adjust your belief system.

You must know what you really want. It must not be what others believe that you should have, but only what *you* want. ***Only you know what's best for you, no one else does.***

Decide what it is that you want.

For the next 90 days, take 15 minutes every day to sit aside, close your eyes (if it helps you to focus) and hold a vision in thought of your desire. Be aware that **you are creating**!

1   For the first 30 days, it may feel to you that it is only a picture in your mind. It may not feel real to you. Your doubt-box will try to confirm that the new beliefs you are forming in your self-box are not real or possible. You will feel the need to stop visualizing, but hold to your vision no matter what and tell yourself: *"That was an old belief. I have the power to create anything I desire."* This may feel strange to you, but even if you don't believe it at this point, keep visualizing it every day and by the end of the first 30 days, you will naturally adjust to it.

At the beginning of the first 30 days, your desire will be a picture in your thoughts and your *infinite intelligence* will naturally start sending you additional thoughts which will turn your picture into a movie. It will send you the details needed toward your creation. Your visions shall become naturally detailed and more specific.

2   In the next 30 days, your emotional guiding system will naturally kick in. You will start **feeling** your way into your vision. Always be aware of how you feel and make sure that you always feel good within your vision. By the end of these 30 days you shall feel that you are really there. It will start feeling real. Your focus will send out a signal to the Universe and you will

begin to know how powerful you are. This will happen naturally with no effort on your part.

3   In the final 30 days, you will start believing that your vision is real. At this time you will receive evidence from the Universe that it is on its way. All around you, you will begin to see signs of evidence on a regular basis. You will see pictures of your desire. You will hear others talking about similar topics. If it's a certain car that you desire, it will start appearing to you in the form of many others driving it or you'll see it being advertised. The evidence will be shown all around you. This will be the Universal law's confirmation that what you desire is on its way to you.

After 90 days, you must now release your desire to the Universe. You must trust the powerful energy that creates worlds. At this time and throughout the entire 90 day process, there is nothing more important than for you to feel good.

You will start feeling yourself transforming into your desire. You will naturally start behaving and taking on the personality that you saw in your vision, and you must keep your frequency at a high level to maintain your communication with your higher power, because when you remain in a good feeling place, you will receive guidance leading you to the path of your desire. You will receive guidance from your *emotions* and guidance from your *infinite intelligence*.

Feel good and hold the powerful awareness that every moment you're in the right place at the right time. There are no coincidences. Feel good and you will be easily guided to the perfect path to your desired reality.

You have the power to create anything you desire, even much faster than 90 days, but it will be of greater comfort for you to utilize the system of time in these 90 days for the beginning of purposely creating your desire.

The *system of time* is a powerful gift that you have and it shall be right by your side working in full force to naturally place your belief system in perfect order to transmit your new reality to the *powerful energy that creates worlds.*

Part Six

The Secret To Freedom

Looking For Answers In
All The Wrong Places

Throughout their physical journey, humans are being guided by their emotions toward the perfect path to their greatest desires. However, most humans let themselves be programmed by others beliefs that they must *face reality*. That belief fills up the doubt-box in their belief system. The one who believe that he must look outside of himself within the rules of society to find the answers, feel the discord within himself. The more they look into the programmed rules for answers, the stronger they will feel the discord.

Most are not aware that the strong discord that they feel is guidance from their own higher power. They search within the rules of man to alleviate their confusion unaware that they are searching for answers in the same place where it began.

The more these people look to those who are trapped within the system of control for answers, the more they are made to believe that there is something wrong within their own minds. Society has fabricated labels of mental illness. That area determined through the eyes of others. Ones' own sense of self holds no weight in this. People are guided by society to seek help within the hands of the doctors within their reality of psychiatry. These social labelers, who themselves live within the eyes of society believe they can fix the minds of others.

The Pattern Of Psychiatry And The Patients

A doctor and his patient

The patient is led to believe that he needs to be fixed and visit the doctor. At the beginning of the appointment what will the doctor do? Ask the patient to repeat their problems. This creates an even stronger discord within the patient, who is being emotionally guided to think different thoughts.

But most believe that the doctors are more powerful than the powers of the Universe, so they do not listen to their own guidance. The doctor will ask the patient to think and talk about everything that is going wrong in his life and even worse, dig deep inside to bring out past thoughts of everything bad that has happened. The patient is unaware that he is now experiencing it again in his present thoughts, which is recreating the frequency to match it.

The patients are unaware that they are recreating the unwanted experiences in their future, perhaps not the exact same experience, but a different or a similar experience within the same frequency level.

The patient is now feeling a stronger discord than before, being guided by his emotions to change his thoughts. The patient's life has not improved and instead feels worse.

Based on the programmed beliefs of society, the doctor will now prescribe the socially appropriate medication needed to fix his patient. And what does this medication do? It numbs the patient. The purpose for the medication is to try to suppress the patient's emotions.

The doctor is now trying to cancel out the patient's guidance system, *which is the most important and powerful tool that his patient holds.*

Don't you think there is something out of place with this picture?

The patient has now fallen further into the realities of others, the reality of the controlled society which has been filling the doubt-box of most people throughout their physical journey. Throughout his life, the patient has been searching outside of himself in others worlds and realities for answers. All along the answers have been within his own being.

When you speak about the unwanted, the discord that you feel inside of you is telling you *not to go there*. Your higher power is communicating with you, telling you to change your thoughts to better ones. That emotion of discord within yourself is letting you know that what you are feeling is creating that same feeling in a future experience. It is informing you that you are creating something unwanted. That you are creating something in your life experience which is contrary to what you desire.

Before you came forth into the physical world, the Universe, which is the bigger part of yourself, made an agreement with the smaller part of you within your physical body that you will be guided every step of your physical journey by the emotions that you feel, leading you to the path of everything you desire.

The Universe already knows what you want and you must trust that your higher power will never guide you to something you do not want. It will always and only guide you to exactly what you really desire.

The only way you can truly find yourself is to know *who you really are* and to know the powers that you hold, to create your own reality. Once you hold this awareness of your guidance within, your path shall be shown to you effortlessly, leading you to everything that you desire.

The War Between Realities: The Need To Prove Them Wrong

Now imagine that the patients found the answers. The *powerful Truth Beyond What Is* resonated with them in a powerful way. The patients found the truth to *who they really are*, where they came from before birth into the physical realm and the awareness of the powerful being that they really are.

The patient now holds the awareness and clarity of the great secrets to live a life of growth, freedom and joy. Aware that he was living his life in others realities and now decides to easily create *his own reality*.

The patient now believes that he found pure happiness and joy and now no longer has a need for the doctor.

At this time upon the planet more than ever before, more and more humans are coming to know this knowledge due to the great awakening of the human race. To know of this knowledge is a good thing but to practice the knowledge is the *key*. It is not enough to *know who you really are*, but you must **be** *who you really are* and use the natural powers that you have.

(At this point, if the knowledge is still not clear to you, I strongly suggest that

after you have read this book, to go through it again and highlight or take notes of all the key points that resonate with you most.)

So the patients have now awakened to the awareness of who they really are, aware that they had strayed from their own path and into others realities. They now realize that they do not need to be fixed because they were never broken.

So now what happens? The patients believe that they don't need to be fixed, but instead they believe that the doctor needs to be fixed because the doctor is the one who is broken. Now they have the need to get out of the doctor's reality and crave the need to bring the doctor into their own reality, to what they now believe.

Do you understand what is happening here? Most humans are led to believe that in order to help someone you need to fix them. Without their awareness, their need to fix someone is a belief that has been created through society. The patients also pick up this belief while looking outside of themselves for answers.

You did not come forth into this physical world to fix anyone, neither to fix the world because it is not broken. Everything is in perfect harmony, including all humans.

Now that the patients have found the great secrets they want to prove they are right and the doctor is wrong. Again they return to the doctor, but this time with a message. What if the patients told their doctor: *"Now I am happy. I found out who I really am. I know that I came from the non-physical realm and I now know how powerful I really am. I believe that everything is an illusion. What has happened to me is not real but was only the frequency of my energy reflecting back to me. Now I know that I am powerful and I know that my thoughts can create anything that I want because I discovered how powerful I really am."*

If society was to teach you all that you truly need to be happy, the doctor's response would be "I am happy for you! You no longer need my services." But instead, what would usually happen, the doctor would label him as suffering from delusions.

Even if the patient feels that he is no longer suffering, the doctor's own reality and programmed social beliefs, believe that the patient is suffering more than ever.

But then the patient, trying to prove his worth and rightness to the society outside of himself will try to prove his theory and with great effort the patient will believe he has succeeded. Then the doctor will label the patient as narcissistic. Who won?

The system of time serves you well as it gives you the time to create, through thought, the magnificent life you came forth to have. Now if someone is taking prescribed medication, I am not at all advising them to stop taking the medication. I am only using examples of how it can be prevented.

What one can do right now is to stop mis-creating a life into a repeated pattern which is the opposite of what they desire. It's easy, much easier than most believe. It is as easy as listening to ones' own guidance and keeping their thoughts in a good feeling place. When someone doesn't feel good, it is always and only because of a thought they are thinking.

Do anything to feel good. Imagine anything that feels good and if that doesn't work, close your eyes and take five deep breaths. Let yourself go and allow your infinite intelligence to send you better feeling thoughts, and it always does.

For one to create their own reality will all depend on how much they want change.

Society's Grand Design Of Powerlessness

The grand design of society, ruled and controlled by man, is designed to restrain its population within a low frequency. That is why negative news is fabricated and reported across the world. The true purpose of this is to program humans to believe that they are all in one same reality, and most importantly a low frequency reality.

People who are operating in a low frequency will have no knowledge of who they really are, and therefore, they can be easily controlled. Society's agenda is for humans not to know how powerful they are, for those who do know *who they really are* cannot be controlled by others. The controlled society is designed to keep all humans in sameness.

Society is ruled by the ones who have, till this day, kept these great secrets from most of the human race. The purpose for their actions is for their own creation and agenda. The battle to prove who's right and wrong is a belief programmed into the human race for the purpose of creating wars.

The controlled society thrives on war. They want humans to fight and protest against each other in order to maintain their agenda of keeping the human race operating at the lowest frequency possible. But the ones who maintain this agenda, like many, have also lost their path somewhere along their physical journey. Throughout this powerful time of the great awakening, those who control others shall reawaken to who they really are or they shall continue down the path to their own powerlessness.

<u>The Luxury Of Silence: Teaching Through Your Example Of Freedom And Joy</u>

It is advised for those *who are awakening to who they really are and* with this knowledge that they hold, to place themselves in the luxury of silence.

When you are thriving and you know that you can be, do and have anything you want and you try to forecast what you know, others may contradict your own beliefs and that may cause you the need to prove yourself which takes you back to where you started.

It is best to practice the knowledge that you have in silence, and once you have reached your life of freedom and everything that you desire, others will naturally want to know what you know.

When they ask you what you know and you are strengthened by the power and happiness where no one can affect the level of your frequency, only then shall be the perfect time for you to teach what you know, to inspire them with your knowledge. You must not try to fix anyone but only inspire them by being an example to others of the great being that you really are.

It is of great importance to never force this knowledge upon another. If you do, it is only because you hold the belief that you must fix them, which shall be of no benefit to anyone. You may reveal what you know only to those who are asking for the knowledge.

Once you have the power of the magnificent being that you really are, you will hold the power of unconditional love, defined as your frequency shall remain in its highest level under any condition.

You will not condemn those who control others, for you shall know that they have only lost themselves within their physical journey. You will know that they themselves have tried to suppress their own powerful emotional guiding system, not knowing the path they have taken and what they are creating. You will understand that they have become so dependent upon the system of society that without their awareness, they will do anything to protect it and defend it. You will know that every single human within this physical world came from the same pure positive energy.

All humans came from goodness and hold the power of purity. All humans are on the exact same mission for joy. If the path of another is not in harmony to what you desire, the power of your emotions will let you know. You must not fight against them. You must let them be who they want to be, because another's reality is no ones' business but their own.

It is not your job to control other people's realities. You shall be guided to simply turn the other cheek and to create your own magnificent reality.

You did not come forth to fix anyone or to fix a broken world. You came forth only to create with the focus of your thoughts, the reality you desire which is your joyous mission. As you live in alignment with the nature of *who you really are,* you will create the change that benefits everyone around you and in return it shall benefit the powerful growth of which you came forth to be.

Who's Right And Who's Wrong?

In regard to the story of the patient and the doctor, what if I asked you, who is right and who is wrong? The doctor who believes that the patient needs to be fixed and brought into their reality? Or the patient who believes that the doctor needs to be fixed and brought into their reality?

Humans did not come forth into this physical realm to try to fix anyone. Trying to fix another is not in harmony with your nature and has no good ending. Trying to fix someone is impossible. Everyone came forth to create their own reality and it is the work of the Universe to match co-creators within their same frequencies.

There is absolutely no right or wrong, no matter the perspective. Before you came forth into this physical world, you knew that you could create anything and that none of it would be wrong. You also knew that if you were to lose *your* path to *your* desires, you would be guided again toward your true path.

No one can do wrong within the eyes of the Universe. The laws of Universal energy are in perfect harmony with all creation.

Everything is an illusion. Everything in the physical realm is a reflection of the vibrating energy that you have created. Everything is a reflection of your own frequency.

What is energy? It is thought. What is thought? It is energy. Everything is energy so everything is thought. Everything operates through frequency and by law two different frequencies cannot co-exist together. This keeps everything in perfect balance and harmony.

The doctor is always surrounded by patients who do not feel good, sometimes by patients who are in severe distress. The doctor's environment is of that same frequency. Two different frequencies cannot co-exist together. Therefore, the doctor has to be operating at the same frequency level his patients are on.

His patients are not to blame for his frequency. By his own magnetic field, he alone has to be operating on that frequency level in order to attract the patients on that level. It is the only way the patients and their doctors come together. It is law.

Many doctors are taught to suppress their own emotions, unaware that they are suppressing the greatest power they were born with. They think they are fixing the patients but instead, they are keeping them in the same frequency level, but in a much stronger way.

In the story, no matter what the patient tries to do to help the doctor, as long as the doctor is operating at that frequency level, there is absolutely nothing that can be said or done to change the doctor because everything is energy and everything operates within the same frequencies. Likewise, there is nothing the doctor can do or say to the patient to change them.

The patient thought he had finally found his path. If he had paid attention to how he felt upon returning to the doctor, he wouldn't have returned because his emotions were guiding him not to go back.

How do you feel when you think that someone needs to be fixed? How do you feel when you think that someone is pure love? They are two different frequencies. It is not the work of humans to direct others back to their true path. That is the work of the Universe. It is the work of someone's *own* higher power.

Everyone has the right to create their own reality. It is every human's birthright. It is the purpose you came forth into this physical realm. There is absolutely no right or wrong to anyone's reality. Only they themselves will know if they are on the right path as, they will be guided by their emotions from their own higher power.

The people that you encounter throughout your life are a reflected vision of yourself to let you know what frequency you are operating on. Everything that surrounds you is what you have created through past thoughts, all images of your own frequency. If someone is not to your preference, you are not to condemn them but instead, you are to turn the other check and thank your higher power for the teachers that came your way.

Do not react to those who you are not in harmony with you. Look the other way. If you do not enjoy what others are doing in their own reality, it is because your desires are not in harmony with theirs. It's that easy. There is no wrong in the choice of another. If you don't like their choices, turn the other way. Do not try to analyze or to ponder on their choices, for if you do, you'll harmonize your frequency within theirs.

Everyone came forth to create their own world and reality. So take the path to your own freedom instead of taking the path to others' realities.

Part Seven

Living The Reality Of Abundance Or Competing With The Illusions Of Lack

Competition is contrary to *who you really are*. One must not compete with other's realities, but instead create their own. Once you are aware that physical action does not create, that only thought energy creates then guides you to the path of the perfect action to take, you shall know that there is no lack of anything in your own reality. As you trust the powers of the Universe, you shall know that you can create through thought, anything that you want.

Competition is a belief that there is a lack of what you want and that you must compete for it. You shall become aware that there is no limit to what you can create. The forces of the Universe are more powerful than any physical action used by man. Through your natural energy of thought, you can create and attract into your physical experience anything that you desire. There is absolutely no lack of anything through the eyes and the powers of the Universe.

As you allow yourself to trust this power, you shall have anything that you want and there is absolutely no limit to what you can have. It must be, for it is Law. Allow all others to create their own reality and focus on magnificently creating your own.

Your own reality is the safest and most joyous place to be, because you have the choice to create whatever you want within your own world.

Tell-a-vision Programming

Throughout history great discoveries were made by those who were labeled as the great master minds. In truth, we are all great master minds in nature.

There was a fabulous discovery that was to prove to the world how powerful human's thoughts really are, evidence that everything is created by thought energy and its frequencies. Evidence that thought energy and its frequencies can create what we want and can be projected into form.

The ability to reflect energy with frequencies into moving images onto a screen was to prove to the world how thought energy functions. It was the fascinating invention of the television.

The word says it all *"tell a vision"*. But throughout history that fabulous invention has been used contrary to its real purpose. It is now being utilized by society as a programming machine for humans.

Again the words explain it all, *"Television Programming."* The news that is broadcasted to the world through the television is for the purpose of programming humans into a reality of sameness, into a reality chosen by those who try to control society. It is to stop you from creating your own world and to program your thoughts according to what they want you to believe.

It functions by controlling your frequency level. The saying "to face reality" is only saying to face others' realities, which is the reality of the controlled society. The broadcast of bad news that you see, is an illusion and not real, unless you focus your thoughts upon it to create the belief of it. It is fabricated from other people's realities. As you are looking at it and focus your thoughts upon it, it is transferred into your belief system for becoming the reality you have created.

You will notice, the more you are connected to *who you really are,* the less you will want to watch the news. For example: How do you feel when you watch countries that are at war? It does not feel good. As you are watching the bad news, you feel bad because your emotion is guiding you, telling you that it is an illusion and not real and not who you really are. Your emotions are telling you that it is not what you came forth to create and it is not the path to your desired creations.

Now after having this knowledge, one may keep watching the bad news thinking that they are strong enough to prevent it from entering into their own experience, but as I have mentioned previously, your brain does not create, your brain is a receiver and transmitter. The Laws of the Universe do not stop functioning for anyone. The same laws operate for everyone. When you focus your thoughts on something for a period of time, it is then naturally transferred into your belief system, even if you are not aware of it.

Because of the powerful frequencies television utilized to project programming onto humans, the faster your belief system will kick-in. Once it is stored in your belief system, it is then transmitted to the Laws of the Universe, informing the energy that creates worlds that it's what you want, that it's official. Even if it is something you don't want. It then becomes the reality of the world around you, the reality of the controlled society, which is programmed into your doubt-box.

The programs are cleverly designed to make sure that you love watching the tube. When you focus your thoughts on television programming, you are no longer creating your own reality, but instead the televised programs are creating your reality for you.

The Hidden Secrets Of The Great One

You are a creator and to assist others is natural for you, because assisting others creates change in your own reality. There is a secret to help others that will benefit your life and the lives of others. It is the secret power of *looking through the eyes of the Universe."*

To illustrate this power that you hold, I will use the perfect example of a person who knew this powerful secret. He was a great master mind who mastered the key to his powerful being. Throughout history this man was labeled as the great one.

He was sharing his powerful messages to many: "Know thyself" which mean to *know who you really are.* "Look within and you shall find your own kingdom and freedom" which mean, that your higher power will guide you to everything that you desire.

Many of the messages that were said by this man have been changed throughout the years and instead of bringing great clarity to mankind, it has brought confusion to so many.

The story of his life ends very much like a horror movie, with details that most would label inappropriate for children when looked at individually. Yet this story is often told to children. It is puzzling to me that some parents do not allow their children to watch violence on television, but then urges them to focus upon the horrific story, sometimes in the form of a very graphic film.

The great one wanted to be remembered for his messages. So why has society made his suffering more important than the messages that he told?

It was designed that way, to create a frequency of suffering within people and to hide the high frequency of his powerful messages. If humans were to wear the great one's messages as jewelry around their necks, instead of the weapon used at his torture, their reality would consist of greater joy. Instead the songs of his torture are sung to the benefit of no one.

Till this day, people wear the symbol used in his name — the weapon that he died from — unaware that it, along with his story, was crafted to represent, *he who reveals the secrets of who you really are and the powers that you hold shall be punished.* It, along with the way the story is told, was created so that humans would fear discovering the powerful beings that they really are and the natural powers that they really hold.

The great one wanted to be remembered by his messages and not by the violent details of his ending and till this day, his torture is programmed by society into the *doubt-box* of most humans, creating fear within humans, if one reveals the secrets, they shall be punished. Because, someone who knows of the secrets of their true powers, cannot be easily controlled by society.

Till this day, many are programmed to believe that the higher power is something separate from humans, but it is not. It is something that you all are.

This man was also known as a powerful healer, which most humans saw as miracles. Healing is a natural power that all humans have. The messages from this man insisted that he was not superior to anyone and all humans upon this planet came forth to this physical realm with the same powers that he holds.

This is the difference between this man and most humans. Throughout his life upon this physical world, he experienced the powerful journey of the great awakening. He not only knew but he **remembered** *who he really was* and the powers he held. He knew where he came from before coming forth into this physical world.

Back then, much like it is now, the controlled society feared this man because of his messages revealing the secrets of how powerful humans are. Why do the rule makers, who are writing the laws of man, till this day, still fear this man? When one remembers who they really are and the powers that they hold, they cannot be controlled by others.

After this man would teach the secret of his powers to heal, his message to them was "Go and tell no one." He was revealing the secrets that were suppressed from the people and also to keep them in a high frequency and prevent them from recreating their illnesses through retelling the story of it.

The Hidden Secrets Behind The Great One's Miracles

To master the key of the great secrets is the awareness of the illusions and the power to create your own reality into anything you desire effortlessly, including financial wealth.

This man was no different than any human upon this planet. You are all powerful in nature and you are all thought energy. This man, who by many, labeled as the great one, knew that everything and everyone was thought energy and used the word "creator" numerous times within his powerful messages.

Throughout history, within the books written by man, the great one's messages have been changed for humans to believe that the "Creator" is a force outside of themselves, a god separate from humans. That is false. This great one knew that everything was only a reflection of ones' own thoughts and of the illusions within the physical realm. That knowledge that he knew, was the only way he was able to perform what most labeled as miracles.

His miracles were performed through the power of *looking through the eyes of the Universe* and everyone holds this power, but most are not aware of it. Once you are aware of this power that you hold and most importantly apply it, there are no words that can express the freedom you shall feel and experience. More and more humans are being led through this time of the great awakening to the *Truth Beyond What Is*, discovering their powers.

The secret of the great one's power to heal was very simple. First you must know *who you really are* and know that everything upon this physical realm is only an illusion created by thought energy. You must know that two different frequencies cannot co-exist together. If two people are together and have different frequencies, one must harmonize with the frequency of the other; meaning, if one feels good and the other feels bad, one persons' frequency will change to match the others' frequency level. Either both will feel good or both will feel bad.

Because most humans have not been aware that they have been living through the eyes of the programmed society, most have been operating in lower frequency throughout their lives; therefore, the lower frequency of a person will usually overpower the other.

You must know, as you practice your ability to maintain in high frequency level, it will eventually overpower anything in lower frequency, meaning, you can become more powerful than all who are operating in lower frequency level. The one, who operates in his pure state of high frequency, is more powerful than millions who are not, no matter what situation or environment that surrounds him. As you hold yourself in a level of high frequency energy, you hold the powers of the Universe.

Most importantly, in order to remain at a powerful high frequency level, you must always follow your guidance and remain in good feeling thoughts, knowing, that there is nothing more important than for you to feel good, no matter what. The Laws of the Universe does not know what you are experiencing. It only reads and operates through the frequencies of your energy.

As the sick, with their desires to be healed, approached the great one, *he did not sympathize with them*; like most were programmed to believe. He did not feel pity for the sick, because he knew, their illness was an illusion. He did not focus on their illnesses, but instead he purely focused his thoughts on *who they really are*. He saw them as powerful beings. He would create, through his focused thoughts, the pure health that they really are.

He knew that everything in the Universe, in either the non-physical or physical realm, functioned through thought energy. He knew that thought energy is the only power that creates change. He had the power to remain in a high frequency level, no matter what his surroundings were. He knew that two different frequencies cannot co-exist together.

He knew that the feeling of pity and seeing someone as ill would bring his own frequency to that level, instead he was able to harmonize the frequency of the sick to his high level frequency of health and purity, and their sickness miraculously vanished.

The great one's frequency level overpowered their sickness, therefore the sick could no longer be sick because their frequency level rose to match to level of the great one's frequency and by law their sickness must vanish.

When you are operating at the same level as the purity of your higher power, you are at your natural state of being, which is a powerful being. Once you reach that level, you can never go back. That's the secret as to how he was able to heal the people. He did not look or focus on their illnesses, but instead he looked at them through the eyes of the Universe and saw who they really were. He did not heal anyone through physical action or medicine. It was the energy that creates worlds. It was his higher power flowing through him that healed the people, the energy of who he really was.

All humans are of that exact same energy. The great one's powerful miracles were but himself, being *who he really was*. Again, he had the power to heal the sick because he did not look at them through the eyes of society but instead he looked through the eyes of the Universe and saw them as who they really are. *That's how simple it is.*

Poverty is a feeling of lack. There is absolutely no limit to anything that you can create, therefore, poverty or lack is but an illusion. One who is living in lack, only lives that way because he is trapped within the illusions of the physical world and has lost his path due to being disconnected from who he really is. He believes the world he sees around him is real and it remains so, as he "faces what he believes to be reality."

Once you return to the natural being of who you really are, you are powerful because your frequency is at a level that reconnects you to the bigger part of yourself in the non-physical dimension. Once you hold the stream of that frequency, you can never be sick, because it is a place where sickness does not exist and a place where lack or poverty does not exist.

The Illusion Of Poverty: Only Thought Energy Can Create Change

All humans are like powerful magicians. As everything is an illusion, you hold the power and the magic to make what you want appear and what you don't want naturally and effortlessly disappear. That's how powerful you are. Once you are aware of *who you really are* and *how powerful you really are,* that's when life really becomes fun. You will feel the freedom and the joy that you can be, do and have anything you want, *effortlessly*.

You did not come into this physical world to fix anyone. You came forth to create your own reality with joy. One may ask, why do so many humans have a strong desire to help others? To inspire someone is different than trying to fix someone. Trying to fix someone is not helping anyone. It is to see them in lack, which will emphasize the power of its growth. No exception.

There is something important for you to know. There is a powerful truth revealing how so many have been misled to a false belief upon this physical planet, a lie that was programmed into most of the human race. This belief has fed the doubt-box within the belief system of so many, perpetuating poverty across the world.

Most humans are programmed by society to believe; "*One must have sympathy for those who are needy*" and even worse, you must bring your emotions into it. "*One must feel pity for the needy.*" That belief has predominantly been taught by society through numerous religions.

That message has led many to great confusion. The belief that one *must feel pity upon another* is a **false belief** and it contributes to the growth of poverty within humanity. If you give money to someone who is homeless and feel pity as you hand him the dollars, you are adding to his illusion of poverty and in return it shall bring no benefit to you.

The belief that you must give in pity, is false. It is contrary to the Laws of the Universe, the laws of energy. Many who have given money to the less fortunate have expected to be rewarded for their good deed, but instead, at a later time, they started noticing a shortage of their own dollars. This leads to confusion as to why the pile of bills are getting higher than the pile of dollars after they have given so much to the needy throughout their lives.

The saying "Give and you shall receive" holds true, but it is misunderstood by most.

Everything including you is energy governed by the same Laws of the Universe. You came forth as a creator and your thoughts are always creating. Understand that everything that surrounds you, every single thing that you see, was attracted to you by your own thought energy.

If you see someone who is homeless, you had to be within that same frequency in order to have attracted them to you. You must have been thinking and focusing on lack at some point. You did not personally create him, but you did attract him into your experience with your own energy and magnetic field. As everything is an illusion, if the frequency didn't match, he would still exist but in a different reality, invisible to your seeing eyes. Everything that surrounds you is but a reflection of your own frequency. The reason that most humans have the need to help others is because they have the need to help themselves, to create change within their own reality.

As you create your reality, without your awareness, in every moment you are observing what you have created around you and you have the need to change your creation to a better creation. This is why most have the need to help others, to change their own reality to a better one. When someone sees a homeless person, it does not feel good, and without their awareness, they are trying to change it to improve their own reality.

But the Laws of the Universe say *"As you create through thought, what you have created shall be reflected to you. The world around you is but a mirror of your own reflection. A mirror that reflects everything you have created through thought. You are to observe what you have created which is reflected all around you. You are to hold a preference as to what you do like and hold your focus in thoughts upon only what you do like, for the continued growth of your own desired creation."*

Most are not aware that they are creators in thought energy and try to take action to fix the lives of others, unaware that they are trying to fix themselves.

It is natural for someone to *want* to help another, but it is not natural to *need* to help another. To want something is to desire something, which is of benefit to your desired creation, but to need something creates lack.

When you give money to someone who's within the illusion of poverty and you feel pity for them, you are contributing to the growth of poverty. This is very difficult for most humans to understand. As you focus your thoughts on a strong feeling of poverty, you are creating poverty.

The action of giving is not what will create change for the impoverished. Only thought energy creates change. Everything is energy and money is also made of energy. If you were to give a homeless person a million dollars in pity, it will only make their problems bigger.

If you give money to another through the low frequency of pity, which is in the same level as lack, it is an absolute promise to you that you shall create more lack for the one you gave the money to and you shall create lack within your own future experience. It is Law. The powerful statement "Give and you shall receive" is a powerful truth, but it has been purposely misled to most humans. Everything is energy and everything operates with energy, including dollars; therefore, it is not the action of giving the dollars that will create change but instead it is the energy of the dollars that shall create the change. Through your thought energy that creates world, as you look at them through the Eyes of the Universe and see them as the powerful beings as they really are, it is the only way you will create change when you are giving them the dollars. It is the frequency of energy within your action that creates the change. Thought energy is what holds the power to create change.

The Giving: See Them As Prosperous And You Shall Receive Prosperity

Now that you are aware of the *power of looking through the eyes of the Universe*, you will know that the only way you can help anyone who is trapped within the illusion of poverty, is to *not* look at them in pity, but to see them as the pure powerful being that they really are and came forth to be.

If you focus on someone's lack, you are creating a stronger reality toward his or her lack and you are also creating lack in your own future experience. As you sympathize or feel pity for someone, it is because you are focused on lack and how does that feel? It doesn't feel good. That feeling of discord is your higher power telling you that what you are focused on is not real. It is not who you really are and not who they really are.

When you feel good, you are operating within the nature of *who you really are*. It is important that, any action you take must be action in joy, otherwise there is no good ending to the action that you take. To truly help someone you must *look beyond* their lack. You must see them as *who they really are* to create change.

Everything is energy, including every physical object that you see, all operating from the same law of energy. Dollars are also energy. It is not your physical action of handing the money to the needy that will help them, but the energy within the intention that can create change. You must focus your thoughts upon them as being abundant and prosperous, with your awareness that their lack is but an illusion. The powerful message "Give and you shall receive" will be evident to you, for as you *give money in the frequency level of prosperity, you shall attract the receiving of prosperity.* If you *give in the frequency level of lack, you shall attract the receiving of lack.* It is law.

As you practice looking at the world around you *through the eyes of the Universe*, you will experience great freedom. You will feel the *energy that creates worlds* flowing through you in a most powerful way.

Part Eight

Disparity: Fast Motion Forward

I will define disparity as unwanted experiences, the experience of contrast, the opposite of what you desire, experiencing the emotions of fear, anger, pain, struggle, lack, disappointment, discouragement or any experience that gives a strong feeling of discord within oneself.

Before you came forth into this physical realm, you knew that it was a world that consisted of disparity and diversity, and you joyfully chose to come forth. As you are a natural creator, you knew that if you were to end up creating disparity, it would not harm you, but instead be of benefit to you and assist you in your creating. This is very hard for most humans to understand. For most, disparity is considered traumatic and painful, filled with suffering and struggle. But you knew before you came forth that disparity was not for the purpose of suffering.

You did not come forth into this physical world to suffer or struggle, to fix anyone or to fix the world. Your *only* purpose for being here is to create the reality you desire and your *only* mission is for joy.

Disparity is an illusion and though it may seem real, it is not. It is created through ones' own thoughts. The feeling of extreme discord within yourself is a signal from your emotional guiding system, your higher power, telling you that the experience you are having **is not** *who you really are*, and is something that isn't real. It is an illusion. The emotion is a strong notification that you have lost track of yourself within the illusions of the physical world and are moving away from your desires.

When you feel disparity, you must focus your thoughts on the opposite toward what is wanted.

When you feel good, your frequency is high and when you feel bad, your frequency is low. Whether your frequency is high or low, you are always creating. What you are creating will match the frequency you are on while creating it.

Your emotions are not creating. Your emotions are only telling you *what* you are creating through thought. As I have mentioned before, two different frequencies cannot co-exist together. *That is why there is nothing more important in the entire Universe than for you to feel good*!

When you feel good, you are connected to your higher power and you will be easily guided through joyous inspirations to the appropriate action to achieve your desires. When you feel good, your energy creates a stream that reaches and allows your infinite intelligence to flow through you in a powerful way.

Feeling good doesn't mean you must jump for joy at all times, feeling good can also be in silence, because it is not the physical action that triggers your connection to your higher power, it's how you feel within, that really matters. You can be jumping all around saying that you feel great but you must *feel* it within your being. That's where your power really is. Repeating positive affirmations are good, but if you don't feel them, they will not benefit you.

Feeling good can also be feeling at ease, feeling comfort, feeling relief or feeling at peace. Feeling excited, joyful, love, eager, playful and thriving are also perfect high frequency levels of emotions, and are effective in maintaining your awareness of your guidance.

The promise that was made to you before you came forth into the physical realm is, as you practice being *who you really are*, feeling the joy and goodness of *who you really are*, you **will** thrive in freedom and prosperity. People around you will see you as happy, beautiful and rich. What will become natural for you, others will see it as magic and miracles. Everyone around you will want to know your secret because it is everyone's desire – and the only reason they all came forth into this physical realm – to have freedom, joy, beauty and financial abundance, which **is,** every human's birthright.

Preventing The Road Blocks To Your Desires

Prior, what you have read about the Triad of Creation in Part Five, which included a 90 day process of naturally and purposely creating your desire into its physical form, many do not pass the first 30 days. This is because, when you follow The Triad of Creation, in the first 30 days into your vision of thought, no matter how good you feel, something may occur in your experience that may make you feel powerful discord. Even if you were focused on keeping yourself happy, the reason that something unwanted may happen within that time is, you are experiencing something that you have created from past thoughts.

Because of the nature of *time*, what you focused on can manifest within 90 days. If there was no such thing as time and if you were to experience trauma, you would be trapped within it. The process of time is a gift. It is your friend and it is always on your side and working for you in full force to assist you in changing your thoughts towards what you desire.

Let's say, you were not aware of The Triad of Creation or the concept of purposely creating what you desire. One day you're in the middle of a painful dispute, either with your mate at home or your child or parents or someone you work with. As you maintain focused on your dispute, the frequency that you are operating on may create something in your future within 90 days, perhaps in a different experience, but an experience within that same frequency level. If you felt anger, an experience that will be equal to the feeling of anger can manifest itself within the next 90 day period.

The next month, you discover this book and you learn about *The Triad of Creation*. You decide to try the process to purposely create your desire. In the first 30 days within the process, you maintain your focus and stay in a happy place, and then, something unwanted occurs. You will know why it happened. You had created it from past thoughts and it has manifested itself in the present, while you were in the first 30 days within the process.

Most humans are not aware that these experiences are illusions, only something they had created from past thoughts.

If that happens to you, don't stop The Triad of Creation process. The best way to avoid future road blocks is not to get caught up in the illusions that present themselves to you. Change your focus to good feeling thoughts as soon as possible and know that the more you stay in your good feeling frequency, the fewer road blocks will appear.

Breaking The Pattern Of Miscreation

Most people develop a habit of reacting to a negative experience over and over again. They react to it and a similar frequency reoccurs in a different experience in their future and again they react to it. Then again something of the same frequency happens and again they react, to recreate it over and over again and then they ask themselves "Why is this always happening to me?"

This is being trapped in an unwanted vortex of miscreation. This creates confusion, convincing people, if they feel really good something bad must happen. That is a very false belief, feeding the doubt-box within the belief system. When one is trapped in a life of miscreation, no matter what they try to do through physical action to change it, it does not change. That is why so many give up on their desires.

If one were to look within themselves, instead of looking outside of themselves, they would find all the answers that they need to live a life of growth, freedom and joy, which is what all humans intended to do as they came forth into their physical world.

If you were to look back at your life, you would be aware of the pattern of miscreation. When you think bad thoughts, something bad happens. You think good thoughts and good things happen. It is so evident all around you. Some people go through 40, 50 or 80 years without being aware of this pattern. Most do not come to this awareness, because they lost themselves, not able to remember _who they really are_ and how powerful their thoughts are, because they are looking outside of themselves, through the eyes of society for answers.

It is important, as you begin the first 30 days within The Triad of Creation process, if something unwanted sneaks up on you, do not react to it. Do not focus on it. Instead, say to yourself. _"This too shall pass. It's only something I've created from past thoughts."_

Do anything to stay happy, no matter what the situation is, and it is an absolute promise that the unwanted shall disappear. Your consistent high frequency level will keep the unwanted far away from you, for the Laws of the Universe state that two different frequencies cannot co-exist together. As you make it through the first 30 days within the process, you will be well on your way to attracting what you desire.

The Hidden Secret: The Quantum Leap

Now that you are aware, disparity is but an illusion within your own thoughts, there is something of great importance for you to know, that shall be of benefit to you. It is a great secret known only by a few, a power that all humans have, a power that was kept secret from most of the human race.

What if I told you, the illusions of disparity can be powerfully used toward the fast motion forward for the creation of what you desire?

Before you came forth, you knew that the physical world was a world of disparity and you knew then, the illusions of disparity could be utilized to create what you wanted in a fast and powerful way. You knew then, the knowing of what you did not want was to bring your awareness to the opposite of it, to the knowing what you do want. So you are here, observing what you have created in your world around you, for the purpose of choosing what you **do** want, from the opposite of what you do not want.

This is how you intended to react to the illusion of disparity. As you experienced the illusion of disparity, you intended to be grateful for the experience, since it would lead to the discovery of what you did not want. Using the system of time, you intended to focus your thoughts on the opposite of the illusion, with a thought vision of the opposite to what you did want within 60 seconds. And with your energy that creates worlds, you would vibrate in a fast motion forward, causing the disparity to vanish and for you to rapidly receive what you wanted. Whether you believe this or not, it is a powerful truth.

The discord that you feel within you as you are in a state of disparity is very powerful. You can feel its strength throughout your entire body, and as you change your thoughts in the direction of what you desire, that strong pull creates your frequency level to elevate at a powerful speed. This is a *quantum leap* into a different reality. Disparity is naturally creating what you desire without your awareness of it.

Through the illusions of disparity, what you desire has already been created and now exists, but because most humans are programmed to believe that the disparity is real, they are trapped within its illusion and their desires are invisible to their seeing eyes, due to their low frequency level.

Within 60 seconds of experiencing disparity, clear all thoughts and let them go. Change the focus of your thoughts to what feels good to you and as you start feeling good, the disparity will disappear and be replaced by the manifestation of what you have created in thought.

Your manifestation can appear as quickly as a few hours or within the same day. That's how powerful you are. The powerful discord within you, shifts the level of your frequency with such speed, that you quantum leap into your desired reality.

However, most humans believe, they must face reality, and developed a habit to react to the illusions of disparity. They believe that they can control it with physical action, rather than being aware that it is thought energy that creates worlds which controls the experience. Therefore, when they experience disparity, they recreate the experience in their future, as they keep focusing on it, which also reinforces their belief system that the illusion is real.

The reason you must change your focus within 60 seconds, is because the energy that creates worlds must know what it is that you want to create, in order to manifest it in its physical form. The longer you keep your thoughts focused on the illusion, the more your belief system will register that it is real to you and it naturally becomes a belief that tells the Universe that, that is what you "want". The Universe does not know the difference between what you are thinking or what you are observing. It only reads your frequency and matches it to what you are focused in thought.

The strong force of discord that you feel as you experience disparity has the power to manifest what you desire in fast motion forward and that strong feeling is your guidance strongly telling you, in that moment, you are creating in a powerful way. It is telling you in a strong way to change your thoughts immediately. The energy that creates worlds does not guide you, it only creates what you are transmitting through your thoughts. Likewise, your emotions are not creating but are only guiding you with the emotion that you feel, to tell you what you are creating.

Most people are programmed by a society who wants the mass population to believe that there is only one reality and you must face it. This is programmed very deeply within the doubt-box of most human's belief system and most have lost themselves within the illusions of the controlled society.

That is why practicing this power doesn't feel natural and is not easy for most humans. But the truth is, it **is** very natural for **all** humans and it is what everyone had intended to do as they came forth into this physical realm. It is a natural power.

The art of manifesting through the speed of disparity has to be mastered. First, you have to know that disparity is an illusion, and only thought energy can create change. You must feel and trust the Universe within the core of your being. You have the power to easily change anything that you want, and through the eyes of the Universe, there is absolutely no limit to what you can create.

Ones' Own Detriment Of Misusing The Power To Get What They Want

Now, what has happened throughout the years, those who knew of this secret practiced its art by purposely creating disparity in order to manifest what they wanted, through the system of the controlled society. That has not been working well for humanity as a whole.

To purposely create disparity, is not in alignment with the powerful beings that you are. This method has fallen into the hands of those who control society, throwing fear upon the masses for the purpose of their own agenda. The news is a strongly positioned tool used to create fear; bad news travels like a virus amongst the mass population for the purpose of creating disparity.

To purposely create disparity is contrary to who you really are. You did not come forth to the physical world to create or experience disparity, however, you knew that disparity was an illusion that might occur and cross your path within your physical journey. You knew that if you were to lose your path within the illusions of the physical world, through the false experience of disparity, you would have the power through your thoughts and guidance, to be led to your natural path again, finding it in a powerful way. As you practice the art of quickly moving from disparity to joy, and utilize it with the power of looking through the eyes of the Universe, you will be on your way to great freedom like you've never felt before.

When someone is in a state of being who they really are – the energy of love, joy, well-being, or any good feeling state, operating in their natural high frequency level – that person is always safe and absolutely no harm can come to them within that powerful state. They hold the powerful force of the Universe within.

When you feel good, your frequency connects you to the Universal stream of infinite power and supply. It connects you to the bigger part of yourself, your higher power, your infinite intelligence. That's why it feels good. Feeling good is who you really are.

When you feel good, you are a natural powerful creator.

Part Nine

Meditation: Placing The Game On Pause

When you sleep, you leave your physical body and awaken from the illusions of your physical realm. You awaken back home in your non-physical reality, the natural state of _who you really are_. When you sleep, you reemerge into your highest frequency of pure powerful energy of love, joy and freedom. Within your non-physical reality, you regain the awareness that your physical world is only a projection of your own thoughts.

Your sleep state is a time to release all your disparity, all your resistant thoughts, to totally release and let go the illusions of the physical realm. It is where you place the game of the physical world on pause, a time to refresh yourself.

Meditation is of the same nature and it is a powerful practice. Many are aware that meditation has many great benefits, but many have also misunderstood its nature.

Meditation is not for the purpose of prayer. It is not a time where you are asking or creating, but it is of great benefit to your creating process. Meditation is a powerful practice, where you release and let go all thoughts of the illusions of your existence within your physical realm. It is a time to place your game of the physical world on pause.

Now remember this, for it will be of tremendous benefit to you! **Meditation also places the system of time on pause**. When you are in a state of meditation, you _do not age_. This is the absolute truth. If everyone knew that, perhaps many would meditate or have the desire to meditate. Though, its purpose is not specifically to stop your aging process, this is one of the **many** secret powers this important practice has stored within its vast treasury of benefits.

The purpose of meditation is to raise your frequency to your natural state of well-being, through the releasing of all disparity within your thoughts.

This is also to your benefit, as the raising of your frequency level brings you to your desires and your desires to you.

The key difference between sleep and meditation is when you sleep, you are not in a conscious awareness, but when you meditate, you bring yourself back to where you came from and to who you really are **while** being in conscious awareness of it. That is why, those who meditate for 20 minutes, can feel as though they have slept for 5 hours or more, reawakening from their meditative state, feeling refreshed.

For those who are new to meditation, it may not be as easy as they thought it would be, because when you meditate, you must release all thoughts from your conscious thinking in order to raise your frequency level to your natural state. But as you practice this art, it shall eventually become easier for you to do. When you meditate on a regular basis, you feel great ease because you are allowing the bigger part of yourself, your higher power, to flow through you and guide you within your physical realm. The flow of well-being that you feel will uplift you to the powers that you hold.

At first meditation may feel like a chore, something you feel like you have to do, but as you meditate regularly, it will feel like a natural practice for reconnecting yourself to the nature of *who you really are*. It will become the most natural part of your existence within your physical journey.

As you have read earlier in regards to quantum leaps, when you are experiencing disparity and choose to release all thoughts within 60 seconds of the experience and then focus on what is wanted, it is to place the system of time on pause, to change realities. That time is a state of meditation but in a shorter version. When you practice your full meditation, you pause the system of time to a greater extent.

As you practice meditation, you are connecting with your energy that creates worlds, which is, your natural energy of love, joy and the knowledge of your infinite intelligence. You release all thoughts, to let your energy that creates worlds flow through you in a powerful way. As you meditate regularly, every moment throughout your focus in the physical dimension, you will feel yourself being guided to your path in a more powerful way, because you are allowing your higher power to be present within you throughout your physical journey.

Meditation is a powerful practice. It will help you to purposely create your desires while using the Triad of Creation process. Reviewing this process, it calls for you to visualize your desires every day for 15 minutes and then release them and go on with your day, maintaining that good feeling place. If you also meditate every day of the 90 day process, it will be easier for you to keep your frequency at a higher level. You will feel yourself being guided more powerfully because you allowed the power within you to be present within your physical realm, and your infinite intelligence and emotions are able to guide you more easily.

During your day, if you feel yourself slipping from your natural state of joy and well-being, this is a perfect time to meditate because it will raise your frequency to a higher level, and it is important for you to keep yourself feeling good most of your day while doing the process and in general.

To meditate, go somewhere quiet and place yourself in a comfortable position. A quiet place where you will not be disturbed is ideal. If you are not able to be in a quiet environment, that's still ok. You just need to be as comfortable as possible. You can be in a seated position or lying down, whatever is most comfortable for you. When you first start to practice meditation, you may fall asleep due to being very relaxed, but as you practice this art more and more, you will eventually remain in your awareness.

Start by closing your eyes and take a very deep breath and release it slowly. You will feel more relaxed. Now release all your thoughts. At first, this may be hard or uncomfortable, but it will eventually become easier and more natural as you practice every day.

Take slow deep breaths with steady inhales and slow exhales. Do this for 15 to 20 minutes. Breathing this way, will prevent you from falling asleep and feed your cells with the oxygen that they want, offering your physical body the well-being it desires.

Do not meditate while are driving or performing a task where you need to focus your attention, because you will be releasing all your focus from your physical world.

You will know that you are in a meditative state, as you will feel a powerful stream of energy flowing through you as you allow your connection with your higher power and your infinite intelligence. This energy is *who you really are*. It is your natural energy that creates worlds.

After 15 to 20 minutes of meditation, you will feel that energy you gathered remain within you for most of your day, and it is important for you to maintain good feeling thoughts to keep your natural energy flowing.

After meditating for 15 to 20 minutes every day for 30 days, you will feel yourself changing and you will be guided by powerful inspirations from your higher self toward the path to your desires. You will be guided to everything that you want with thoughts that will flow through you as powerful ideas, answers to questions and solutions.

You will witness the Universe yield to you, pieces of your desire, delivering signs to you that your every request is on its way. Everything will happen naturally and effortlessly, because when you meditate, you allow the Universe to flow through you and be present with you within your physical journey.

Visualization: The Alignment Of Your Desires

As you begin to purposely create your desired reality, you begin with a vision in thought of what you desire. Do the visualization process described in *The Triad of Creation: The 90 Day Process* every day for 15 to 20 minutes and you will naturally experience less and less disparity through your everyday life experience.

Most believe that the visualization process is the beginning, the start of creating what they want. It is not. The purpose of visualizing is to establish the level of frequency needed to bring your desire into its visible physical form.

Throughout your physical journey, as you experienced disparity, without your awareness, you already created what you wanted. That force of discord that you felt within your body, which was similar to a shock, was actually creating a pause within your creating process. Without your awareness, you already had a vision in thought of the opposite of that disparity, which is what you wanted. But because of your state of shock, you did not remember that for a fraction of a second you went back to who you really are.

So what you wanted has already been transmitted to the Universe and has been created. It has not become visible to you, due to your frequency level that was still aligned to the level of disparity. Throughout your physical journey, every single experience of disparity, without your awareness, has caused you to create what you wanted and what you want already exists, but it is not visible to you until you align your frequency level to match it.

Everything that you want has already been created. It is real and it is in the invisible realm. The Universe already knows exactly what you want, even if you are not consciously aware of what it is that you want. That is why you are always being guided by your higher power, because it already knows what it is that you want, which is not always consciously known to you within your state of the physical realm.

So you see, when you do your 15 minutes of visualization, it is not to create what you want, because it is already created. It is to align yourself with the frequency level of it, to make it visible to you.

Your physical brain does not create any of your thoughts. When you do your visualization, it is your infinite intelligence in your invisible non-physical realm that is sending you the thoughts of what you have already created without your awareness. Whatever you desire has already been created, whether you believe it or not. What you desire is only waiting for you to align yourself with its frequency level.

As you receive this knowledge within *The Truth Beyond What Is,* you will know that you alone have created the disparity in your life, as your physical journey has led you to know what you do not want for the purpose of choosing what you do want. Now, doesn't it make sense to you, that one cannot know what he wants until he or she experiences what they don't want?

Prior to being aware that you create your own reality, you led yourself in a journey through illusions to purposely experience disparity in order to create what you do want. So as you visualize your desires every day, you are affirming to the Universe that you are preparing yourself for the receiving of what you want, which it has already been created.

However, once you reawaken to *who you really are*, and deliberately choose to create wellbeing within your life, you no longer need to experience illusions of disparity to create what you want. If you purposely visualize your desires every day, you will be exposed to less and less disparity for, when you visualize, you are communicating with the Universe that you already know what it is that you want. Once you begin constructively creating your reality, without the need of experiencing the opposite of what you want to know what you do want, you will experience less and less disparity.

It is very important that you hold your frequency at a high level as you visualize. Feeling a good high level frequency **is** the purpose of visualization. You must feel good when you visualize your desires because you do not want to invite anything opposite. You do not want to repeat the disparity. This is why the art of meditation is of great benefit to receiving your desire, as it raises your frequency and connects you to your higher power, opening the door to your powerful pathway.

Before you begin visualizing, be in a fully aware wake state, not in a state of meditation. Remember, meditation is for the purpose of releasing disparity which temporarily places physical creation on pause.

If you are in a low level of frequency, it is best to take a deep breath and release all thoughts before you begin to visualize. As you feel your frequency rise, it will be a good time to enter into your place of visualization. You do not need to close your eyes and focus; you just need to feel good and to allow yourself to receive the visions of your desire.

Remember, what you desire has already been created and already exists. Your infinite intelligence is sending you the thoughts of your visualization, for you to align with its frequency, so you can see it and then allow yourself to enjoy it in its physical form.

Message In Closing

Life is only a game. You only came forth for the fun of being here. It is not at all a serious or mysterious journey. It was not your intent to come forth to find yourself or go through hardship, for lessons well learned. It is not at all a world where one is to live in spirit alone and shut themselves off from the world's physical or material nature. If that was the case, you wouldn't have chosen to come forth into this physical or material realm. It is a physical world and you came here for the pleasure and fun of creating any tangible thing you desire, with no limits or boundaries.

Your physical body is not for the purpose of working hard to create what you want, like most are programmed to believe by society. Your magnificent body consists of physical senses for the purpose of feeling the joy and comfort of what you have created and physically manifested through your thought energy. Once you reawaken to *who you really are* and to your nature of purposely creating, that's when your physical journey really becomes fun.

Your only work upon this physical planet is to focus your thoughts on what you desire, to feel good and to allow yourself to be guided by your powers within to the path of all you desire. That is your only work. It is the absolute truth. The most powerful **key** you can hold is your awareness that absolutely nothing is more powerful in the entire existence of the Universe than for you to feel good. It is the magical **key** that unlocks the path to all your desires. It is the powerful *Truth Beyond What Is*.

Quotes In Closing

Life Is A Game

"Life is a fun and simple game of Hot & Cold. When you Feel Good, you are getting hotter to your desires. When you feel bad, you are getting colder from your desires. The better you feel, the closer you are. The worse you feel, the further you are. Have fun."

The Agreement

"I shall Guide You with every Emotion that you Feel" You said "I will live in Joy." The Universe has fulfilled its Agreement and kept its Promise to you. Have you fulfilled your agreement and kept your promise?

The Master Who Holds The Key

"The Master who holds the KEY is not the one who creates, for you are all Creators in nature. It is the one who holds the Awareness and the Clarity of Who He Really Is and of the Powers that which he Holds who has Mastered the Art to Create on PURPOSE."

The End

it is not, but only the Beginning of Your Awakening to the Powerful Creator that You Really Are

The Author Marie Poirier

"Who I thought I was is, raised in Canada, and like most I was born in an institution called a hospital and registered to the controlled system through birth registration with no choice in the matter. And like most at a young age, I was then registered to the next level of institution called the school system, which through deep breaths, I decided to break free from, due to a tremendous discord I felt within the programmed system of beliefs. Shortly thereafter, I decided to break away from the religion of my upbringing which contained teachings of guilt, fear, and that all humans were to be labeled as "born sinners".

It was then, I began searching for the truth. At the age of 17, I discovered the writings of Napoleon Hill, Norman Vincent Peale, and Wallace Wattles and later in my life, Anthony Robbins, Jane Roberts, Earl Nightingale, James Allen (philosopher) and Thomas Troward. These and many more marked the beginning of my powerful journey.

Living through a failed marriage and the life of a single mother, I was determined for financial success and so I brought on the creation of new product developments which reached the success of global demand. Yet still, I was driven to exhaustion and then trapped within the system of poverty. But then the worse of all my experiences was when my daughter was taken away through initiatory force by the hands of the controlled society ruled by man due to their fear of the secret knowledge that she held, knowledge that has remained a secret by society till this day. It was then, I came to the great loss of all hope.

But if I would have known then the truth that I know now, I would have known that the life of struggle and pain is an illusion; it is for the purpose of finding the awareness and clarity of the powers that we hold through our thoughts, which are guided by our emotions, and leads to the shocking truth of *who we really are.*

From the painful loss of my daughter, it was then a passage through an unexplainable powerful experience that I received the answers that I had formerly been looking for in all the wrong places. It was the Powerful answers to life's mysteries. It was my awakening to the remembering of *who I really am*, where I came from, the purpose I chose to come forth into this magnificent physical planet of time, and where I go upon leaving this physical realm with the awareness that there is no such thing as death. And with this powerful knowledge that which I hold, life is no longer a mystery to me. It is now my powerful knowing that once one remembers *who they really are* and masters the key of the powers that which he hold, he shall live a powerful life of growth, freedom and joy.

It shall be for it is Law.

Printed in the United States
By Bookmasters